# Rapid Idea Generation:

*How to Create, Innovate, Conceive, and Invent From Scratch [Second Edition]*

**By Peter Hollins, Author and Researcher at** petehollins.com

## Table of Contents

Table of Contents ............................................. 5

Chapter 1. Introduction ................................ 7
   History's Greatest Polymath? ................... 9
   The Psychology of Creativity ................. 17
   Creativity Is the Key ............................... 30

Chapter 2. Creativity Building Blocks .. 39
   Mental Locks and Blocks ....................... 42
   Building Block 1: Nothing Is New—And That's a Good Thing ............................... 49
   Building Block 2: Inspiration Is a Myth; Creativity Is a Skill ................................. 56
   Building Block 3: Combine, Combine, Combine ................................................. 64
   Building Block 4: Distance Yourself .. 68

Chapter 3. Rapid Idea Generation ......... 77
   Tactic 1: 100 Ideas List .......................... 85
   Tactic 2: Forced Randomization ......... 91
   Tactic 3: Thinking More "Plainly" ... 100
   Tactic 4: Idea Box ................................. 105

## Chapter 4. Rapid Idea Generation Part 2 ............ 113
- Tactic 5: Wear Six Hats ........................ 114
- Tactic 6: Use Intentional Constraints ............ 122
- Tactic 7: SCAMPER It ........................... 132
- Tactic 8: Multitask (Yes, really) ........ 144

## Chapter 5: Beyond Convention ............ 153
- Einstein and Combinatory Play ........ 154
- Dali and Chasing Hypnagogic Sleep 164
- Da Vinci and the Habit of Prolific Notes ............ 168
- Murakami and King and Living Through Routines ................................. 171
- Dr. NakaMats, the Most Unconventional of All ........................... 176
- Edison and Why Nothing is Sacred. 180

## Summary Guide ........................................ 187

## Chapter 1. Introduction

James Dyson had a real problem with vacuum cleaners.

Back in the 20th century, a household vacuum cleaner worked by rolling over the carpet, grabbing dust with brushes attached to a cylindrical mechanism, and then sucking up that dust and storing it in a bag that was connected to a pipe. When the bag filled up, you had to take it out and replace it with a new one. In many ways, it seems crude, especially when you consider that we will soon have self-driving cars on the road.

Dyson absolutely loathed changing out the vacuum cleaner bags. He assumed, quite correctly, that other people hated it too. It was a filthy business; dust got everywhere, and often it left matters just as messy as when he had started. He decided he was going to try and find a way to create a bag-less vacuum cleaner. The big issue, of course, was how this cleaner would dispose of the dust. For a while, Dyson didn't have any ideas.

One day, Dyson was at an industrial sawmill. He noticed that it was relatively *clean* for a sawmill. He discovered there were a couple of large cones that not only collected the sawdust, but removed it from the air. These machines were called "cyclonic separators."

Dyson thought this principle could be adapted to work in household vacuum cleaners, so he fashioned a crude cyclone model out of cardboard and Scotch tape, connected it to his normal vacuum cleaner, and went about sweeping the home. He found that it worked extremely well.

He went to work building prototypes and trying to line up financing. After fifteen years of trial and error, Dyson's cyclone-powered, totally bag-less vacuum cleaner hit the market. Eventually it became a tremendous success. Now the vacuum cleaner bag is nearly extinct, and no housecleaner ever has to live with getting lint all over his or her hands.

Dyson solved his bag problem by assessing a situation, coming up with a theory, being curious about other industries, experimenting on his own, and finally producing the ultimate solution.

He probably didn't realize it at the time, but in finding a workable answer for bag-free vacuuming, Dyson was emulating a few of the most well-known creative problem-solving principles, ones that Leonardo da Vinci used to great effect. To be clear, this isn't a book about da Vinci's life, but he just so happens to be the archetype for creativity and out-of-the-box thinking for so many of us that he's a fantastic role model to analyze. It's from following his lead and mindsets that we can start to become more creative in our own ways.

### **History's Greatest Polymath?**

Leonardo da Vinci, born in 1452 in Tuscany, Italy, is arguably the most famous and accomplished polymath in the history of the world, as well as someone recognized for massive creativity. A polymath, sometimes colloquially referred to as a "Renaissance" man or woman, is a person with deep expertise across an impossibly wide range of subjects and disciplines. Science, math, the arts, politics, culture, history—you name it and he cultivated an interest in it and likely gained a level of proficiency.

Polymaths have deep and ongoing interests in multiple areas. When a problem comes along, polymaths solve it by tapping into their knowledge in different subjects. They're relentless about gaining knowledge and putting it into application. Galileo (1564–1642) was a polymath who explored astronomy, mathematics, physics, and engineering and who basically gave us the modern scientific method. Benjamin Franklin (1706–1790) was an expert in politics, science, and philosophy who, between inventing bifocals and discovering electricity, helped found the United States of America. It seems that there is a clear pattern between a mastery of multiple disciplines and creativity.

Da Vinci, though, is the model from which all subsequent polymaths are borne. His list of accomplishments is staggering, and the variety of fields he mastered is beyond belief.

*Anatomy.* Da Vinci reshaped what human beings knew about themselves. He was the first person to create detailed views of the internal organs of the human body. He made casts of the brain and ventricles from a deceased ox, paving the way for such models of human organs. He was the first to describe the S-shaped structure of the human spine. He completed numerous dissections of both human and animal bodies, meticulously documenting and drawing everything he saw. Imagine how valuable those diagrams were, coming from someone so artistically skilled. Even today, da Vinci's many illustrations of human anatomy are still necessary studies.

*Innovation and invention.* Da Vinci's foresight was incredible. He came up with drafts of several inventions that were finally brought to life almost five hundred years after he lived—the helicopter, the parachute, the military tank, the robot, and scuba gear all sprang from ideas first put forth by da Vinci. And that's just a partial list. He had a particular interest in military and defense inventions, and biographers have speculated that his various artistic endeavors were only meant as stopgaps so he could find more work in warfare.

*Architecture.* Da Vinci was fascinated with large-scale construction projects and served as a consultant to builders of his time. He designed a system for canal locks that wound up being extremely close to the types that are used today. He even dove into urban planning with his conception of "the ideal city."

*Art.* Da Vinci painted a couple of masterpieces you may have heard of: the *Mona Lisa* and the *Last Supper*. His iconic *Vitruvian Man* drawing of the human body is as much a piece of art as a scientific explanation. Da Vinci also revolutionized the use of landscapes in his art and was an early innovator in the use of oil paint. He was a sculptor as well.

*Science.* Da Vinci's expertise made him a key figure in the development of studies in several different sciences. He was the first to speculate that fossils would prove that earth was far older than those of his time believed. He made detailed depictions of plants that influenced how botany was studied. He made intensive studies on the motion of water. He designed mills, machines and engines that were powered by water. He even designed a musical keyboard that played bowed strings.

Occasionally he slept, we can assume. But how did da Vinci accomplish everything he did? What made him so influential in so many different disciplines that continue to be a part of our everyday lives?

Was it truly a level of creative genius that few have been able to aspire to ever since? Yes and no.

Author Michael Gelb explored possible reasons in his book *How to Think Like da Vinci*. Gelb examined a multitude of da Vinci's achievements and notebooks and speculated on a few facets of the polymath's character and traits that could explain why the Renaissance man was so prolific and visionary.

What's inspirational about Gelb's list is that the traits that defined da Vinci's genius are all inborn human elements each of us can improve with just a little more awareness. Even if we can't conceptualize a flying machine or an iconic piece of art as da Vinci did, we can easily emulate his approach to improve the quality of our minds and what we produce. Thus, it can be said that we can indeed think *like* da Vinci and learn the fundamental mindsets he possessed, albeit perhaps not as effectively or intensely.

Gelb identified a few traits in particular that he felt were responsible for da Vinci's creative prolific habits (I'll present my own in the following chapter).

*Insatiable curiosity.* Da Vinci was driven to know the truth in all its aspects. He was curious about scientific principles. He was intent on finding out what worked. He would ask "why" until he truly comprehended. Indulging his own interest led him to visualize solutions to problems that generations in the far-off future would encounter. When you are curious about something, you will attack it from every angle and never cease trying to solve it, and that can lead to spectacular creativity and resourcefulness.

*Seek knowledge through experience.* People in da Vinci's time weren't used to challenging long-held beliefs through their own investigation; governmental and religious forces discouraged the population from questioning anything they decreed. After all, Galileo Galilei, not quite a contemporary of da Vinci's being born in 1564 while da Vinci died in 1519, came into great conflict with the church over his concept of heliocentrism, the notion that the earth revolved around the sun and was not the center of the universe.

Da Vinci wouldn't have that restriction. He sought to answer his questions through firsthand experience and wanted to get as many perspectives on a situation as he possibly could. It's only when you are able to challenge the so-called rules and conventional ways of thinking that, like da Vinci, you can be creative.

*Embracing the unknown.* Da Vinci didn't seek quick certainty; he sought truth. In doing so, he had to deal with ambiguity and uncertainty—which is just how he liked it. He went into situations and lines of thought without feeling he needed a definite answer. He knew that adhering to a strict code of safety and belief would keep him from exploring the world, so he circumvented the rules and accepted the unfamiliar.

*Balancing art and science.* More than anyone, da Vinci held logic and imagination in equal importance. He balanced the two apparent opposites and saw how both approaches were important in decoding truth. By holding art and science in equal esteem, da Vinci obtained a more complete overview of the world that fascinated him. It's likely this mixture of interests that was in part responsible for his degree of insight and genius.

His imagination was so powerful that inventors born centuries after da Vinci used his notes and observations to build their own creations. For us, this could mean looking for answers to practical questions through the arts—using drawings to explain complex functions, or music to describe the functions of a beating heart.

Da Vinci's motivations were so broad and all-encompassing that his ability to channel them into focused work and results almost makes him superhuman. But the factors that drove da Vinci are ones that almost all other humans on earth can emulate, and they serve as a kind of blueprint for creative thinking.

## **The Psychology of Creativity**

Still, attaining that kind of creativity is difficult for some of us to imagine. Worse yet, some of us feel that it is impossible. Creativity is popularly considered—not entirely accurately—more of an impulse than a function. Often, creativity is tied to the notion of natural talent that only certain people possess. That assumption is also incorrect.

Just like analysis, memory, and communication, creativity is a complex function administered by several parts of the human brain. Researchers have spent myriad hours in lab environments trying to determine where creativity comes from and what parts of our anatomy control it. While they've made progress and come up with some firm determinations, perhaps the elusive nature of creativity has transformed its mystery into certain myths about the brain's role.

*The Left Brain/Right Brain Myth*

This idea is certainly responsible in large part for perpetuating the notion that creativity is inborn. In the 1970s, neuropsychologist Roger Sperry worked on a study, the findings of which gave rise to the theory of the split brain. Sperry's work suggested that the two hemispheres of the human brain control different realms of thinking: the left side handles logic and analysis, and the right side enables intuition and subjectivity.

When these findings were published in the media, casual readers seized on the dichotomy of "left-brain/right-brain" people. Scientific, mathematical, and practical people were thought to be dominated by their "left" brains, whereas creative, artistic, and imaginative people were controlled by the "right" side. This catchy contrast is impressed upon many of us as scientific fact.

But it's a myth—or, more accurately, an overly simplistic explanation of how the brain actually functions. Sperry's experiments involved animals and humans who had their corpus callosums severed. The corpus callosum is the thick bunch of fibers that connects the left and right hemispheres of the brain and serves as the conduit of information between the two sides. Some epilepsy patients had their corpus callosums surgically cut to lessen the effects of seizures—so only one side of their functioning would be impaired during a seizure.

So in someone with a severed corpus callosum, if the right eye (left brain) sees a table, the left brain says "table," and everyone's comfortable with the fact that the table has been correctly identified. But if the left eye (right brain) sees a table, the right brain says, well, probably something unintelligible. We're not sure what.

Each side of the brain controls the opposite side of the body: the left brain controls the right eye and vice versa. Sperry discovered that when test subjects covered their left eye—controlled by the right brain—they were able to process and accurately name certain items their right eye saw. But when they covered their *right* eye—controlled by the *left* brain—they couldn't remember any of the items they saw with their left eye.

Through his studies, Sperry isolated certain functions that the left and right brains performed and how they applied to language, math, drawing, interpretation, speech, and so forth. From these results came a very overgeneralized picture that the left brain is analytical and the right brain is creative. Even though Sperry himself cautioned against making that rash distinction, when it was discovered by popular culture, it was too catchy to resist.

From these results came the theory that the two sides of the brain handle entirely different kinds of processing. The left side deals with numbers, language, and reasoning. The right side oversees emotions, creativity, and intuition. If it sounds like a leap in logic, that's because it is.

The truth about the brain is a little more complex, and Sperry himself insisted we remember that. Yes, the left and right sides of our brain handle different *functions* and collaborate with each other through the corpus callosum to get thinking done, but researchers found that both sides do roughly the same amount of activity in all people. A mathematician's right brain doesn't just "turn down" when they're working, and a composer doesn't simply suspend their left brain when they're writing.

A great example of how the two halves of the brain work together is in learning a language. The left brain, analysis central, identifies the alphabet and pronunciation of certain words, but the right brain picks up on intonation, stress, and emotional content. The two sides collaborate to determine the whole meaning of a word or phrase in a certain language.

So you're not a left-brain or right-brain person—no one is. Creativity engages all aspects of the brain and calls upon different functions in both sides. Understanding that could be the key to unlocking your creative possibilities. Creativity is indeed something learnable, and it doesn't particularly matter how good you are at math.

*Default Mode Network*

As you might suspect and have experienced firsthand, the brain has multiple types of functioning modes. When you're sleeping, for instance, the brain has a very specific focus and set of duties. When you're trying to solve a difficult math problem, you activate what's called the *executive attention network.* This mental mode helps your brain hyperfocus and accomplish a specific goal that requires concentration and ignoring potential distractions.

As you might also predict and hope, there is another type of mental mode that assists in creativity, abstract thinking, and the generation of ideas. It's just not one that you can push yourself into. Rather, it's the opposite—you must relax yourself into it.

If a solution is outside of your brain's familiar experience—which is shaped by your beliefs, culture, and biases—your conscious mind will most likely never find it. The conscious mind deals too much in fact and the present, which stands in stark contrast to abstract thought and conceptual thinking. An analytical search for a solution can comb through the entire content of your mind's "known," but not outside of it. Novel answers reside outside of your mind's known box, and the subconscious is the first place to look.

When you allow your brain to integrate new information with existing knowledge on a subconscious level, it can establish new connections and see patterns not obvious to your conscious mind. Creative solutions and ideas are more likely to bubble up from a brain that applies unconscious thought to a problem, rather than going at it in a deliberate approach with your frontal lobe. When your thinking brain is inundated with information and analysis, it doesn't have the opportunity to connect concepts or make creative leaps.

Science shows that your brain's resting state, called the default mode network (DMN)—which is activated when you stop thinking about something specific and just veg out—is the best place to park a problem. In the DMN, your brain does some of its best, wisest, and most creative work. Research from Raichle and Snyder in 2007 demonstrates a predictable pattern of neurological activity that's your brain's go-to state when it's at rest, not focused on anything in particular, or actively engaging with its environment. It's associated with experiential thinking, mind-wandering, emotions, past encounters, and intuition. The imagination network is used in situations like brainstorming, painting, daydreaming, or devising a new recipe. Yes, this is where you might consider most creative thinking to occur, while execution and analysis occur in the other mental networks.

This mental state is also where ruminating and worrying take place. Hey, no one said that it wasn't going to have its downsides. The harder and more cognitively demanding a particular task is, the less the DMN is activated. We'll discuss later on how to use this DMN to your advantage.

*Creatives: Crazy or Genius?*

When some of us think of legendarily creative people, we occasionally make the very dubious observation that many of them were, to some degree, crazy. The meaning of creativity infers the ability to invent something out of nothing, to call into existence something that wasn't there just a second ago. That involves going outside the info-processing boundaries of the brain and just making things up—which some people might consider "crazy."

To be sure, there have been some artists and creators who suffered from a variety of emotional disorders. Charles Dickens, Ernest Hemingway, Virginia Woolf, Tennessee Williams, and Leo Tolstoy all dealt with clinical depression at some point, according to certain studies (which were, it should be noted, highly contested by some). Researchers also determined that many—but not all—creatives endured difficult life experiences like losing their parents, social rejection, or physical handicaps.

But no evidence has conclusively proven that mental illness is a contributor to a creative person's productivity. A study of over a million Swedish citizens, conducted over a span of four decades and completed in 2012, found that artists were *not* likelier to have psychiatric ailments. They were, however, found to have an unusually high number of *relatives* who suffered conditions like autism, schizophrenia, bipolar disorder, or anorexia nervosa.

Artists themselves typically had more highly developed *schizotypal* traits. Despite the name, having these traits isn't quite the same as having a schizophrenic disorder. In fact, almost everybody on earth has these characteristics.

Schizotypal traits are mainly positive. Generally speaking, they involve what motivational speakers would call "thinking outside the box": unique perspectives and experiences, nonconformance, maybe even a fanciful belief in magic. There *are* some unseemly schizotypal traits as well—cognitive disarray and difficulty feeling pleasure—but by and large, the schizotype reflects the positive aspects over the negative.

A 2008 study by British scientists Mark Batey and Adrian Furnham found that positive schizotypes were associated with character traits like confidence, insight, resourcefulness, diverse interests, and even sexiness. They were also oriented toward doing at least one creative thing every day.

Then, of course, there's the precuneus.

The precuneus is a part of the superior parietal lobule, located between the left and right hemispheres of the brain. There's still some mystery about how it actually functions in relation to other parts of the brain, but it's known to have several very complex jobs: memory retrieval and processing, environmental analysis, cue processing, organizing mental images, and pain reaction.

How the precuneus relates to creative people is that they can't turn the darned thing off. Neuroscientist Hikaru Takeuchi found in 2011 that creative types could not suppress their precuneus. They were unable to filter out inessential brain activity. While this might sound like Takeuchi said creatives were cluttered with meaningless thoughts, what he actually meant was that they had more access to creative stimuli and could put ideas from different networks together. And in 2013, Austrian researcher Andreas Fink found that there was a direct link between the inability to suppress the precuneus and higher generation of original ideas.

What this all means is that the key to creative thinking is to let as much information into one's brain as possible in order to make connections and associations between different elements. Even if that cognitive process results in strange, outlandish, weird, or—say it together—"crazy" associations, those connections often produce the most creative ideas. This can be great for generating hundreds of ideas at once if properly harnessed, or result in mental chatter you can't escape that completely drowns out coherent thoughts. It can be a double-edged sword.

I don't want to speculate on whether da Vinci was crazy—but we *do* know that he came up with blueprints for the airplane, the parachute, the bicycle, the guided missile, and even the snorkel multiple centuries *before* they were physically invented. He could only generate those ideas by letting his precuneus run wild and thinking as creatively as anybody ever could. If that's crazy, then I'll have *more* crazy. Just know that the side effects for such heights may be more than you bargained for.

*Creativity Is Good for Your Health*
Despite a dubious link to mental health, being creative not only produces solutions, new thought processes, bold ideas, or a nice quilt: it actually has great benefits to your physical health.

The *American Journal of Public Health* noted that engaging in a creative pursuit is a great way to relieve stress. In fact, you don't even have to physically *do* something creative to de-stress—the journal claims you just have to *watch* somebody doing something creative or see the results of their work.

Creativity impacts the brain in much the same way that meditation does: by focusing on mindfulness, being in the moment, and reflecting on internal process. Whether it's sewing, painting, building a garden, or watching a movie, both the act and the mere engagement with creativity naturally stimulate a sense of calm.

Creativity also promotes increased functionality of the brain. It encourages production of new neurons that are crucial to the central nervous system. According to the *Croatian Medical Journal*, art therapy has been found to be an extremely valuable tool in repairing brains that have been injured in some way, helping to rewire some of the functionalities that have been damaged. CNN reported that middle-aged and older people who take up artistic pursuits were 73 percent less likely to develop the mental impairments that lead to dementia.

Considering those physiological benefits to creativity, it's a wonder that *anyone* would deem it something that should only be reserved for one's spare time or weekends. It's a trait that needs to be engaged *more*, in as many life areas as we can use it. And certainly, in view of how much he produced, da Vinci obviously created nearly twenty-four hours a day.

## **Creativity Is the Key**

You probably don't need more convincing as to the benefits and virtues of being able to think more creatively on a consistent basis. You can see that it's led to some of the greatest innovations in history, and it can keep you healthy and happy.

And yet, there is more. Truly creative people can apply their faculties of asking "what if?" to every single area of life, specifically using their imaginations to solve problems. This makes sense when you think about it: any problem you have is in a way a failure of imagination, i.e. the failure to conceive of and access those ideas and concepts that constitute a solution. Solving a problem requires something special of us. It asks that we think something we haven't thought before, try something we haven't tried before, or imagine a perspective that we currently don't hold. What could be more creative than that?

Let's talk more concretely and look at exactly what we mean when we say "problem" before we talk about "problem-solving." A problem is the experience of realizing that there is a gap between what is and what you wish the case to be. All problems can be framed as a tension between the reality and what you desire. You are hungry, want food but don't have any food;

you wish that you had a garden without any pests to bother you, but you have aphids and want to be rid of them; you have two equally important invitations for Saturday night and don't know which one to go to, but you must decide; there's a car heading right for you, making it so that your desired future reality and the future reality it is suggesting are in conflict…

You get the idea. Right in its very definition, we see that problems are whatever they're defined to be. The way we conceptualize of a problem is more important than the problem itself—in fact, our manner of thinking about a situation *is* the problem. Therefore, addressing how we engage mentally with reality is the best and only means to arriving at a solution.

We can think of *four main types* of problems.

The first type is where we know what the problem is, we know what needs to be done, but for whatever reason we can't motivate ourselves to take that action. The problem here is our resistance to actually bringing about the solution, or our procrastination, fear of change, or lack of motivation. Examples could include dragging your feet when it comes to going to gym to achieve your fitness goals, struggling with quitting any kind of addiction, or simply being lazy when it comes to taking those actions required to achieve the outcomes we know we want. Solving these problems is more a matter of finding the right mindset to manifest the solution that is already understood and identified.

The second type is also where we know what the problem is, but to solve it requires more knowledge or skill than we currently have. Here, it's not so much a question of motivating ourselves psychologically or removing unconscious resistance or limitations, but rather being more systematic in seeking out the information or expertise we currently lack to solve our problem.

You might be trying to choose between two potential careers, but don't have enough information about either to make an informed decision. Your solution is therefore to seek that information. If your problem is you have a hole in your roof and you don't know how to fix it, the solution is to seek a roofing expert. If your personal accounts are in shambles and you're having trouble filing your tax return, (part of) your response will be to create better techniques to store and organize your data. Underlying all these solutions is simply adopting the right attitude, and systematically thinking about what's needed, what you have, what you don't have, and what you want. It's drawing a clear path between your current state and the state you want to be in.

Creativity can also be substituted here for expertise or information. You may put together a makeshift roof repair solution using what you know to buy yourself more time. You may not know anything about taxes or accounting, but you certainly use your creative thinking skills when you recall that you have a friend whose partner is an accountant, and consider what you could offer them in return for some expert advice.

A third type of problem is again where we know what the problem is, but the solution we need requires a total shift in perspective, a new pair of glasses to look through, a complete out-of-the-box approach. This ability to reframe and reconsider is fundamentally a creative enterprise. This is because there is actually no new information needed or uncovered—there's only the need to look at the same information in a different way. We don't change the problem in front of us, but *ourselves*, and how we perceive that problem.

By being creative, we ask, "How is the question itself affecting my perception here? What other question could I ask?" We give ourselves the opportunity to reframe, rearrange and restructure. We become curious about our very ability to perceive and organize information, and ask how we can change or become better. A classic example: your "problem" is that you have an irate customer who left a scathing review of your business on a public site. But look at it another way: this person is in a prime position to give you honest and very valuable feedback about what's not working in your business, so you can improve and avoid the outcome in future. What a gift! With a shift in perspective, the problem is no longer a problem.

Finally, the category of problem that creativity is best able to solve: those problems that are actually unknown and need to be identified in the first place. This is the space where we challenge our assumptions and habits, brainstorm new ideas and get a better handle on the realm of what's possible. The trick with hidden problems is that they need to be uncovered first, and this can only happen with a large dose of creative thinking. As an example, imagine that a couple starts experiencing problems in their relationship but don't really know why. They only know they don't get along anymore, and things aren't working. Is it a loss of "spark"? Old resentments? Is their "problem" actually perfectly normal for their stage of relationship? Does their communication style need improvement, or is it simply that they're no longer as compatible? By going to couples' therapy, for example, they can begin to ask pointed questions to get to the root of the issue—*creative* questions that they may have never thought to ask before.

Takeaways:

- Creativity is something we all want, but how can we even define it? Perhaps we can describe it best by looking at someone who appeared to embody creativity—Leonardo da Vinci. He possessed a few traits in spades that may have been the keys to his success: curiosity, experimentation, mindfulness, embracing the unknown, and balancing multiple disciplines in both artistic and scientific endeavors alike. We can emulate these traits, which means creativity is a learnable quality. The spark of insight that James Dyson used to create his revolutionary vacuum cleaner was a distillation of some of those traits.

- Some of us, however, are constrained by one of the most longstanding myths in psychology—the myth of hemisphere-specific functionality. In other words, people believe that they have talent in only the left hemisphere (logic, rationality) or the right hemisphere (creativity, art). This leads us to believe that we are inherently destined for a lack of creativity. Basic neurobiology proves this to be untrue. Moreover, three specific modes of thought all span both hemispheres. We're all two-hemisphere thinkers!

- There have often been associations between creativity and mental illness. Do these claims hold any water? Yes and no. There is certainly a correlation between the two groups, but there is nothing to suggest that one causes the other. A major factor may be the functioning of the precuneus, a brain structure that filters out mental chatter from your consciousness. Thus, if it filters poorly, your head will be filled with endless chatter that you can't turn off. This can be fertile ground for creative ideas just as easily as "insanity" from not being able to experience silence.

- We already know we want creativity, but it also has health benefits. Creativity has been shown to reduce stress, improve brain functioning, and create similar soothing effects to meditation. This is achieved through keeping an active brain.

- Last and certainly not least, creativity gives you the tools and keys to solve problems. This might seem self-evident, but it's not always that we need creative *solutions*; sometimes we need to creatively define the *problem* as well. We frequently will need to look at matters from a completely different perspective to get where we want.

## Chapter 2. Creativity Building Blocks

Artist, architect, inventor, engineer, scientist—these are just some of the roles Leonardo da Vinci embodied in his life as a prolific creative. There is no question he was an accomplished originator, with his creative genius springing mainly from the general traits fleshed out by Michael Gelb. From an intense curiosity to a highly sharpened sensory awareness, these traits made da Vinci a fountain of ideas and solutions so remarkable we're still talking about his genius centuries later.

In the same way that Gelb recognized those traits that spawned da Vinci's extraordinary ingenuity, we can also identify practical mindsets that could serve as the building blocks for a more abounding sense of creativity. These building blocks will structure your thinking so that you start to view the world in a new light, stirring you to be more creative subconsciously and practically. Contrary to popular thought, creativity isn't reserved only for those born with an artist's hand or an inventor's imagination. It's something you can learn to better develop in yourself by having the right mindset to nurture it.

What usually hinders people from maximizing their creative potentials isn't the lack of creative capacities, but having a mistaken mindset on what creativity is all about.

Take for instance Terry, a graphics artist contracted by a company to design a new ad for their food product. He has two weeks to deliver the output. The first day after getting the project, he sits at his work desk with a pencil and a blank piece of paper to try to sketch out some ideas for the ad. Nothing comes to him.

An hour comes and goes, and still nothing. He decides to leave the project alone and go do other things instead, thinking to return to it once inspiration strikes him. He never touches anything related to it again; he only waits for his muse to appear and grant him a flash of genius before he gets down to work. Hours become days, and days pass without him getting anywhere with the project. The deadline arrives, and Terry has nothing to deliver for his clients. He might feel like a complete failure and constantly fret that he just doesn't have what others in his field seem to naturally possess.

What Terry failed to realize is that inspiration is a myth. To wait for it before getting down to work is sentencing a creative venture to doom. Creativity is not something that calls for a waiting game; it's a skill that needs active effort and discipline to harness. Say Terry gets another week to complete the project this time.

Recognizing that he can't just rely on flashes of genius to come up with creative ideas for the ad, he resolves to set a fixed number of hours every day to work on the project whether or not he feels motivated or inspired. To stir up his creative thoughts, he does research on the company and their products, looks at their previous ads, and notes down the interesting ideas he comes across. He finds that inspired ideas strike him while actually working. Eventually, he's able to design a creative ad that he's proud of and that brilliantly captures his client's vision.

His experience proved to Terry that creativity has to be treated as something that requires persistent effort and discipline, just like any other professional skill. This is just one building block of creativity that can boost the quality of your creative output as well. This chapter will delve deeper into this notion of disciplined creativity, as well as discuss more building blocks to help you exhaust the creative possibilities in your own life.

## **Mental Locks and Blocks**

Before we delve into the building blocks, it's worth mentioning what keeps us from opening up and taking advantage of the techniques in this book.

Yes, creativity is a subtle, living, breathing entity that can be a little hard to define at times. But we also have plenty of research showing us exactly what it's made of, and how best to nurture it within our own lives. Before we can realistically ask what creativity is and how to develop our own abilities, we need to be truthful about everything that's standing in the way of our doing so. Many people have vague resistances and fears about creativity that they never really take the time to articulate or examine. They simply say, "I'm not creative," and never look into the matter further.

As part of our mission to become more creative, we need to do the hard work of naming all the mental blocks that keep us from our natural creativity. And this is in essence the shift in perspective: *We are all creative*, and it is natural to be creative. What is *not* natural are all those thoughts and beliefs that tell us we are not allowed to create, that we are bad at it, and so on.

Many of us have hidden (or not so hidden) beliefs about the world and ourselves that make it impossible for us to be creative. It's only in addressing these beliefs directly that we can release them and give ourselves the opportunity to enjoy our creativity, to feel good about thinking new things, and to feel comfortable with the creative process.

Roger Von Oech's famous book, *A Whack on the Side of the Head!* deals with all the *mental locks* we hold on to that keep us from novel, fresh, out-there thinking. Creative thinking belongs to all of us—creativity is curiosity, joy at life, a thirst for mastery, an appreciation of yourself and others, a zest, a faith in one's own mental faculties... most of the reason we don't constantly dream up new and creative ideas is not because we're fundamentally incapable, but because we artificially limit ourselves with the "mental locks" outlined below. Read through some of these to see if you can recognize any in your own thinking. Most of them are completions of the sentence, "I can't be creative because..."

### ...I might be wrong

Conventional schooling teaches us there is a right way and a wrong way—and those who are wrong might get punished! A junior at work might see a novel solution to a problem the company is having, but because it doesn't *look* like the right kind of answer, he has no faith in it and doesn't share. He may also hold back because he fears his suggestion might ultimately prove to be incorrect.

Advice: Let go of the need to be right. In fact, strive once in a while to deliberately be wrong, just to prove to yourself that it's not the end of the world. Look for the second-best answer. Even better, look for as many answers as you can, or change the wording of your question so that you get more answers than you thought possible.

Finally, give your ego a check and remind yourself that it's not a genuine threat to be wrong in life. In fact, it's evidence that you've ventured off the beaten track and are actively growing and changing. Get used to failure and risk. Invite them in and see what you can learn from them. If you can drop the negative feelings that you've "failed," you can open up new avenues to explore—how can you become better next time?

### …It doesn't make sense/isn't logical

New ideas often don't. This belief is really fear of the unknown in disguise. To find something truly innovative, we have to leave behind our old habits and conceptions, and risk trying something new—which might seem odd, uncomfortable or even frightening at first.

Advice: Forget about logic. Do you think the theory of gravity seemed *sensible* to anyone at the time? Did the greatest artists ever have critics praising them for how logical and sensical they were? Embrace imperfect, "fuzzy" logic and trust the process. Everything that's currently considered logical is thought to be so precisely because it is not creative.

### …I don't want to break the rules

Sometimes, to build something new, we have to clear away what's already there, and this can feel destructive and a little dangerous. You may decide you want to move countries entirely, but a little voice in the back of your head is telling you that you're not really "allowed" to do that; you're only allowed to solve your problems in the ways others have already solved theirs, and you should feel bad for thinking too far out the box.

Advice: Have courage to be a rebel. Ask uncomfortable questions if you must. Rules can be helpful—but decide for *yourself* how you'll determine their helpfulness; don't let others or your own fear decide for you. *The rules are the box.* That's the opposite of our goals.

### ...It's not practical

Many people allow their creativity to die under a heavy burden of practical obligation. They judge themselves harshly, thinking that creative thinking and ideas are flimsy and frivolous. Have you ever heard a talented person utterly condemn themselves by deciding not to pursue their art simply because it couldn't pay the bills or they "don't have the time"?

Advice: Give yourself permission to simply *ask* new questions. You don't have to act. Yet. We all need to be hard-nosed and practical sometimes, but can you carve out a moment in every day to entertain possibilities—*any* possibility—without saddling it with the burden of being perfectly workable and risk-free? If you can't do this, you're stopping yourself before you get to the starting line.

### ...I don't want to be wishy-washy
For some of us, ambiguity is something to be feared and avoided, even though it's part and parcel of creative thought. Fearing being unclear, miscommunicating or things getting chaotic and out of hand, we reign in creativity for the sake of clarity. A woman may have a brilliant idea to share but trash it prematurely because she's having trouble articulating it just yet to her colleagues, and she believes only perfect ideas are worth exploring.

Advice: Go easy on yourself and sprinkle a little humor into the creative process. Remind yourself that it's OK to make mistakes.

### ...Being creative is silly
Some people genuinely think that play is only for children, and that adults who have too much fun in life deserve deep suspicion and a stern talking-to. Do you know anyone who acts as though life is meant to be super *serious*, joyless and full of unrewarding work and nothing else? Fearing that creativity is too frivolous points to an underlying distrust of pleasure, and its role

in the creative process. If a manager keeps suggesting his group's brainstorm ideas are "stupid" and shuts down playful or silly suggestions, what is he communicating to his team?

Advice: Enjoy yourself. Not only is having fun allowed, it's almost required for a proper outcome. Take your time and don't rush. Consider that fun and enjoyableness are key ingredients to fresh, new, innovative ideas. Don't stifle yourself by being your own creativity police!

**...I'm not really an expert**
Do you have the belief that you're only allowed to tackle ideas in your specific niche, and you're not allowed to tread on other people's turfs? We all specialize in life, true, but sometimes the answer to your problem lies outside your ordinary scope of affairs. Someone may feel like, for example, if they're trained in the medical field, they can only ever offer opinions, ideas and concepts that are medical in nature, even though their curiosity and the situation are asking them to step outside that role. Similarly, a person without training in an area may feel unqualified to provide their view, even if their being an outsider is precisely what allows them to see things in such a refreshing way.

Advice: Don't limit yourself. Drop the labels when you can and simply become curious about the underlying similarities across situations, despite their surface differences.

**...I'm not a creative person!**
Perhaps the most common mental lock—and totally untrue. The only difference between a creative person and person who believes they're not creative is a little faith. If you insist that you're not creative; fine. Try something new anyway, just because. Surprise yourself. Follow a random whim and laugh about it. Let go of expectations for the outcome. A man might consciously tell himself, "I feel silly doing this, but I'll give it a go" and unwittingly open a tiny creativity door in himself.

Advice: Give yourself the opportunity to prove yourself wrong. The smallest of risks, the tiniest thoughts or creations all count. Do something different and watch to see what happens!

## **Building Block 1: Nothing Is New—And That's a Good Thing**

One of the ideas that inhibits creativity is the notion that it must always come as a flash of genius or an amazing "aha!" moment where they discover something totally new and unheard of in the history of mankind. They sit at their desks all day, trying to will their muse to magically appear and inspire in them an otherworldly idea, and when nothing new or *inventive enough* comes to them, they feel frustrated and grow more and more convinced they are simply not cut out for creative work. Eventually, they abandon all attempts at trying to lead a creative life, leaving it to the artists, inventors, and "true creatives" to do the hard task of coming up with something totally original, preferably a masterpiece of sorts.

But here's what those great artists, inventors, and creatives have known all along: *nothing is completely original.* Every new idea has roots from somewhere else or is an outgrowth from a more primitive "parent idea." What we call "original" actually came from preexisting themes and ideas that have only been reimagined or combined in new ways. Yes, we might even use the word *derivative.*

As artist Austin Kleon put it, no idea exists by itself in a vacuum. Thus, the challenge of creativity is not so much about dreaming up a truly original thought, but about figuring out which preexistent ideas are worth stealing, borrowing from, modifying, or altering. As the adage goes, "Good artists borrow; great artists steal." This quote has been attributed to Pablo Picasso, as well as to T.S. Eliot, though the idea itself is likely to have originated elsewhere—thus proving its own point that nothing is truly original.

So yes, nothing is new. But why is that a good thing? It's because knowing that nothing is completely original takes the pressure off of you to squeeze your brain dry trying to come up with something totally innovative. It allows you to redirect your mental energy from the hugely challenging but futile task of sparking an original thought to the more manageable charge of looking at what's already present and then rearranging its elements in new and interesting ways.

See, you don't have to produce the ingredients from scratch yourself; you already have the ingredients all around you, and now you just have to cook up something with them. You don't need a specific muse or point of inspiration—they exist all around you if you look at them in the right way. In a sense, this realization also points you in the right direction. Look at existing things, ideas, and concepts and use everything around you in plain sight as inspiration; *don't* look into an empty void and hope for something completely new and novel.

Creativity thus has little to do with conjuring new things from thin air and everything to do with uncovering new ways to see and use what is already there. You have to stand at a point where you're aware of the elements and ideas that already exist and you see the potential of those to be made into something else, something worthwhile, valuable, and actually feasible.

This point is what Steven Johnson describes as *the adjacent possible* in his book *Where Good Ideas Come From*. For an idea to work, it almost *has* to be founded in something that already works—that's the type of validation you need for its value as an idea. The adjacent possible is what you can realistically expect an idea to turn into after moving forward. Being creative means being able to push an idea into the next stage it has the potential to evolve into.

Take for example the automobile. It could not have come into existence unless the wheel, the horse-drawn carriage, and the combustion engine were already invented. Each of those prior inventions must have occurred first, in succession, before the time of the automobile finally came. The automobile was the adjacent possible that grew out of those earlier creations, and it would have been impossible to invent it before the invention of the wheel or the carriage. It can certainly be said to be adjacent possible to the horse-drawn carriage!

But of course, it would've still been possible for someone to imagine the automobile—a wheeled machine powered by steam or fire to transport people—before the idea of the carriage came to life. In fact, many great inventors had dreamed up machines before it was possible for them to be constructed in reality—thus earning even these great minds the reputation not of being creative, but of being too ambitious and in some instances just plain crazy. Da Vinci's own primitive helicopter comes to mind—a spiraling, cork wheel of a vehicle that may or may not have ever been actually tested.

Creativity is about building on what is already there. It's filling in the gaps between what exists and what can exist but doesn't yet—that is, being able to perceive the adjacent possible and turning that possibility into reality.

Take for instance how various security systems have evolved and built upon one another. The door lock-and-key system is an ancient technology grounded in the idea of a person having the sole means to open something by possessing an object with a unique structure (i.e., the key) and matching the lock to the access point (i.e., the door). Newer initiatives have built on this old idea ever since.

Now, locks have so been fashioned such that the "object with a unique structure" doesn't even have to be something separate from the person—it's the person himself, with the "key" being his fingerprint or his retina scanned at the access point. This idea has also evolved to apply to lock mechanisms for mobile phones and even start-up systems for cars. It's only a matter of time before someone invents the next big thing building on these ideas by contemplating its adjacent possible and turning it into reality.

A great innovator of the tech age, Steve Jobs, agreed with this view of what creativity is all about. As he put it, "Creativity is just connecting things. When you ask creative people how they did something, they feel a little guilty because they didn't really do it. They just saw something." Creativity is less about originating something and more about spotting the potential of certain things or ideas to be combined in a fruitful way. So cut yourself some slack and allow yourself to peek into what others have already come up with. Open your eyes and soak in all the great ideas you can from the world around you. Decide which ones are worth keeping, then figure out connections and combinations among them that would be likely to work. Remember that even great artists and inventors have stolen ideas from somewhere, and you would do well to take a leaf out of their book.

Recognizing that creativity is less about coming up with something from scratch and more about seeing the old in new ways, you take the first step toward obtaining a new set of lenses to help you see all the creative possibilities around you.

## **Building Block 2: Inspiration Is a Myth; Creativity Is a Skill**

One of the most widespread destructive myths about creativity is that you have to wait for inspiration to strike before you sit down and do creative work. We imagine great poets hearing the whispers of their muses as they write their exquisite rhymes, novelists being woken up by imagined characters in their heads suddenly inspiring them to write an epic plot twist, and inventors experiencing a flash of genius while taking their shower and then running out naked shouting "eureka!" In fact, the myth of "eureka" moments is damaging in itself.

Basically, you've heard that there is a prerequisite to creativity and that you can't will it into existence. This is what creativity looks like to most people, and though popular, such a view is simply misguided.

Recall how, in an earlier example, Terry waited endlessly for inspiration but ended up suffering the consequences as he saw the deadline pass him by with inspiration still nowhere to be found.

Of course, such moments of inspiration and sudden sparks of insight may in fact occur—but they do so very rarely, if at all. Many of the instances we hear about turn out to be myth or legend, such as Isaac Newton sitting under a tree, getting hit by an apple, and then conceiving of the concept of gravity.

Sitting back and waiting for such divine moments to come to you before you decide to do any work is guaranteed to leave you unproductive, frustrated, and even angry at your imagined muses. There is this wholly romantic view of the creative life being a carefree existence where you simply close your eyes a few moments, and then feel your creative juices push your hand to paint inspired brushstrokes on a canvas. But the reality of what a creative life truly looks like is far less dreamy than that image. Creativity is not a supernatural power; it's a skill.

And like any skill, creativity needs to be developed and cultivated through consistent, dedicated, and painstaking practice. You can't just sit back and listen for your muse's whispers; you'll have to create the lines yourself. You can't simply wait for a flash of genius; you'll have to manufacture it yourself—and the good news is that you can.

So just how do you manufacture your own inspiration?

First, get comfortable with the feeling of *confusion*. One of the reasons why people sit around all day and wait for inspiration to strike is that they're not looking forward to working in a state of confusion, of not knowing what to do or where to take an idea. It's uncomfortable and, most often, decidedly not pleasurable. The thought of getting a flash of genius that informs you exactly how to do things in an instant is way more attractive than getting your hands dirty and trying to find the information yourself. The latter just seems too messy, and this is what hinders most people from progressing with creative work.

And so if you are to have any hope of achieving your creative goals, you'll need to learn how to persist through the mess and confusion that any worthwhile creative task necessarily involves. Such persistence is what Michael Gelb, in his book *How to Think Like Leonardo da Vinci,* calls *confusion endurance.*

This concept teaches that in order to be creative, you must have the ability to endure the confusion that comes with the task. This confusion may come as a result of not knowing where to start, being perplexed at how to attack a problem, having a muddied view of what you're trying to achieve, wondering what resources are available and relevant to the task, and the like. Confusion endurance is all about being able to stay with a task and persisting in trying to work out a creative solution instead of just abandoning it when things get too difficult. It's about being able to persevere when you have the uncertainty and confusion of juggling multiple balls and not knowing where they will all land. It's the feeling of coming to a fork in the road with ten paths and having to analyze each one.

Say you're standing in the middle of a messy room filled with boxes upon boxes of clutter to move and organize. It's an uncomfortable feeling to be surrounded by essentially chaos. You'll need to get creative with organizing the interior of the room in order to have enough space for everything you need to store inside it. If you don't have the ability to endure the chaos created by the mountain of disorganized stuff around you, you'll never stay with the task long enough to figure out a viable solution.

Hence, you'll need to have enough confusion endurance to withstand the initial disarray you're faced with, as well as the personal bewilderment you may feel from not knowing where to start or how to get the task done. As you learn to sustain your efforts to categorize, organize, and structure the things around you, you also get closer and closer to the creative solution you need to accomplish the job.

Confusion endurance is about having the stamina to get down to work and keep working through tough times, instead of just waiting for inspiration to strike. See, creativity isn't the art of passively expecting a magical lightbulb moment to inspire you. Rather, it's finding ways to turn the spark on yourself, even if it means rubbing two sticks together for quite a while, so to speak. It's hard work.

You'll need to develop the self-discipline to just get started and get working, even if you don't feel inspired or motivated in the moment. Because here's another creativity building block that professional creatives know and the amateurs don't: inspiration and motivation come *after* you get started.

As Pressfield highlights in his book *The War of Art*, the main difference between the amateur and the professional is that while the former talks, the latter acts. While the amateur chatters incessantly about the many brilliant creative ideas he's dreamed up over the years, the professional simply puts his head down and his butt up, silently working until he actually delivers something concrete and substantial.

The professional finds his inspiration and motivation *while* working, as he feels his ideas build on each other in better and better ways the more he keeps persevering with his creative efforts. It's in the middle of the process that he experiences a rush of creative juices flowing, as he opened himself up to imminent inspiration by simply starting.

This again shows how creativity is a skill that needs dedication and discipline to master. Before you can reasonably expect to create something worthwhile, you'll need to put in the hours and the effort laying brush on canvas and pen on paper and putting ideas to the test. You'll need to show up to work even if you don't feel like working, because that's what a professional does. While the amateur has her head in the clouds, fantasizing about the accolades she'll get after she's created something grand, the professional has her feet on the ground and her hands busy working on project after project until something sticks.

Of course, not every single one of the projects a professional attempts is destined to be gold. In fact, many of them are bound to be junk. Out of the ten paintings an artist does, only one may end up in the showroom. Out of the fifty pages an author writes, maybe only five are actually useable. Nonetheless, these professionals know that all the junk created in the process of painting that one piece or writing those five pages was to be expected and was even necessary.

Often, it takes going through a lot of wrong strokes and bad ideas first before you can know how to best develop a creative project. But remember the prior point—that creativity almost always builds upon something else. You are building your own foundation to draw upon when you simply put your head down and get started with producing and creating.

In the pursuit of a creative goal, bear in mind that freely occurring inspiration is a myth. If you want a great idea to "strike" you, you need to work for it and at the very least put yourself in a position for it to "strike." Much like in other professions and fields, it's hard work and perseverance that matter most in the arena of creativity. Stop waiting around for inspiration and instead start working. The ideas will come to you while you're hard at work, and the only way they can keep coming and get refined is if you persevere with working. Creative outbursts are not magical gifts from some temperamental muse, but rather the reward of a hard day's work.

## **Building Block 3: Combine, Combine, Combine**

The third building block of creativity is the *Medici effect*. Business consultant and author Frans Johansson describes the Medici effect as the emergence of new ideas and creative solutions when different backgrounds and disciplines come together. The term is derived from the 15th-century Medici family, which helped usher in the Renaissance by bringing together artists, writers, philosophers, mathematicians, and other creatives from all over the world. Arguably, the Renaissance was a result of the exchange of ideas between these different groups all being in close proximity with each other in 15th-century Florence and Rome.

Johansson proposes that in the modern business world as well, the Medici effect is the key to best meeting client needs and maximizing profits while minimizing costs. Believing that all new ideas come from merging existing ideas in creative ways, he recommends utilizing a mix of backgrounds, experiences, and expertise in staffing to bring about the best possible solutions, perspectives, and innovations in business.

And the same holds true for creativity in general as well—pulling in knowledge from different disciplines and relating things from various fields are powerful tools for generating creative ideas. A common object in one field may be an extraordinary tool in another. A perspective or approach might be commonplace in one discipline but revolutionary in a different one. A conventional concept in one discipline may have new and interesting applications in a different domain.

For example, creative ways of implementing traffic rules have pulled ideas from not only electronics, engineering, and information technology but also from visual arts, psychology, and advertising. It's a familiar concept in psychology that people, when making decisions, rely on not only rational information but also emotional cues. Utilized in implementing traffic laws, this concept has led to the innovation of using smiley faces in traffic lights to get more people to respond better to them.

The advantages offered by pulling together knowledge and resources from multiple disciplines to aid problem-solving are evident in the findings of researcher and professor Brian Uzzi. Analyzing over 26 million scientific papers published over the last several centuries, Professor Uzzi found that the most impactful have been those done by teams with members coming from an atypical combination of backgrounds. Another investigation he conducted also revealed that top-performing studies cited an atypical combination of other studies, often pulling in at least 10 percent of their citations from fields other than their own.

Thus, to be creative, you'll need to evoke the Medici effect by broadening your perspective to encompass different disciplines and not being afraid to wander outside your current area of focus. In other words, you'll need to think outside the box. Poke your nose into other fields and pull from them ideas that might work in combination with what you already have. By bringing in knowledge from other disciplines, you introduce a fresh take on your creative venture and give yourself the best chance of coming up with remarkable innovations and solutions.

It is perhaps no coincidence that we still speak of da Vinci and his polymathic tendencies—perhaps it is due to those very tendencies. At the very least, he was an accomplished painter, sculptor, engineer, architect, and anatomist. He also possessed keen interests in ornithology, machinery, and ciphers. He is the prime example of how different disciplines can come together, synergize, and spit out creative work that is revolutionary and innovative. It is also no coincidence that the Medici family was one of da Vinci's prime patrons during his lifetime.

Albert Einstein also utilized this concept in his method of *combinatory play*, which we will cover in a later chapter when we delve more deeply into his specific tactics for creativity and innovative thinking.

## **Building Block 4: Distance Yourself**

We've mentioned the widespread myth of creativity being an inborn trait gifted to just a few special individuals. Such a view is not only discouraging to those who think they weren't born with such a trait, it's also not accurate. Creativity is not the domain only of a few gifted ones; it's a skill anyone can develop by having the right perspective and thinking tools.

The final building block of creativity is learning how to create *psychological distance* between you and the creative task. This is the concept that when we are too closely invested in something, we lose the ability to see clearly and we become trapped by our own perceptions. Just imagine how easy it is to give dating advice to friends, and even easier yet to give it to strangers. Now, how difficult is it to apply that same advice to yourself? That is the power of psychological distance and, conversely, the dangers of being too closely invested. (Does this also remind you of the *default mode network* from the first chapter?)

When you are too invested, emotionally or otherwise, you are unable to take yourself out of the equation.

Psychological distance may be achieved by separating yourself in space, in time, or in probability. In other words, you can increase your creativity by imagining things as far away from you (distancing in space), projecting things as happening further into the future (distancing in time), or considering things as not very likely to actually happen (distancing in probability).

You may also create psychological distance by imagining things as concerning someone else instead of you (distancing in person). The premise is that by increasing psychological distance, you will represent things in your head in a more abstract way, better enabling you to imagine unusual connections, unexpected combinations, and more unique innovations. When you're invested or attached, you can only see the limitations, and you will operate from a place of fear or protection. Distance frees you from these constraints.

This idea has thus far been proven true by studies such as one conducted by Lile Jia and colleagues from the Indiana University at Bloomington. Their research looked into the effect of spatial distance (distancing in space) on creativity. The participants of the study were given a creative generation task in which they had to enumerate as many different modes of transportation as they could.

One group was told the task was developed by Indiana University students studying in Greece (distant condition), while another group was told it was set by Indiana University students studying in Indiana (near condition). The result showed that participants in the distant condition came up with more numerous and original ideas than those in the near one.

Such a result was replicated in their second study, which tested the participants' abilities to solve problems that required insight. As in the above outcome, participants who were told that the insight problems were developed by a research institute "around 2,000 miles away" (distant condition) were able to solve more problems compared to two other groups: those who were told that the problems were set by an institute just "two miles away" (near condition) and those who were given no information about location (control condition). The problems thus seemed to be easier to solve the further away they appeared to occur.

Additionally, previous studies on psychological distance concerning time and probability have shown similar results. As revealed by a series of experiments, participants who were asked to imagine working on a task a year later (distant future) performed better on insight and creativity tasks than those who imagined working on the task the next day (near future). Participants were also able to solve more visual insight problems when they believed they were unlikely (low probability) to face the full task.

The results of the above studies thus show that psychological distance sparks more creative thoughts. When you think of a problem as being further from you in terms of space, time, or likelihood, you get to extract yourself from a limited, concrete view of it and assume a more objective and abstract perspective. When we include ourselves in the equation, we become constrained by our own limitations. This shift frees your mind to think of other possibilities beyond your current situation, and thus enables you to arrive at more creative ideas and solutions.

So the next time you feel wrung out of fresh ideas for a creative venture, try to consider the task as coming from somewhere far away, or maybe think about how it might be tackled if it occurred in a distant place. You can also set the problem as happening in the distant future, say fifty years from now, and imagine how it might be solved then.

Alternatively, think about solutions or events related to your task that would probably never happen in reality. Or mentally pass on your problem to a friend and imagine how they would solve it. All these methods would create the psychological distance you need to think more abstractly and thus creatively about your creative endeavor.

Say you have to think of all the new methods you can for cooking without using gas-powered or electric equipment. To stimulate your imagination, create psychological distance by thinking of the task as a problem faced by someone living halfway across the globe from you. How might this person solve the problem of cooking with such limited means? Would they think to use certain materials, tools, or the natural environment, maybe?

You may also project this problem as something you face fifty years from now. Can you imagine more modern means of cooking you may have access to decades into the future? How might technology have evolved to accomplish cooking without using gas or electricity? By creating such psychological distance, you would surely rouse your mind to come up with more creative solutions for your problem.

So there you have it—the four building blocks of creativity. First, recognize that nothing is new. That's a good thing because it means you don't need to think up something out of nothing; you need only see what's already there in a new light. Second, treat creativity like a skill that requires discipline and endurance instead of like some magical quest for inspiration. Third, learn how to combine disparate elements and pull knowledge from different disciplines. And fourth, try to distance yourself from the problem or the task to gain a new perspective.

These four building blocks will change your view of the world around you and of creativity itself, so you can become more naturally creative.

Takeaways:

- We learned that Leonardo da Vinci abided by some strict mindsets in his quest to be creatively prolific. This chapter contains some building blocks and builds upon those mindsets, while seeking to dispel some myths surrounding creativity that might be holding you back.
- It's helpful to first explore what keeps us from being creative, what keeps us inside the box, and what keeps us from tapping into our inner well of ideas and zaniness. Roger Von Oech calls these

barriers mental locks, and they are all internal dialogues that are at odds with creative thinking and rapid idea generation. In essence, they make us think too safely and conventionally, while controlled by a healthy amount of self-doubt and self-consciousness.

- First, nothing is new. Everything is derivative. Most things are merely a result of being adjacent possible. And this is a good thing! Take the pressure off yourself to completely reinvent and revolutionize, and then redirect your attention to what already exists and how you can use it for yourself. Simply look around first before sequestering yourself in a quest to be 100 percent innovative.
- Second, inspiration is a myth. There is no muse. There is no flash of insight or epiphany. These things do not exist. Well, at least plan for life without these things because you cannot control them. Thus, approach creativity as a skill you must cultivate, and practice it like any other skill. Key to this is gaining confusion endurance.
- Third, creativity comes from combinations of element. This is called

the Medici effect. What is commonplace in one field might just be revolutionary in another, so again, redirect your attention to what is plainly visible already instead of seeking a moonshot.
- Fourth, psychological distance is necessary for creativity because when we leave too much of ourselves in a thought process, we become constrained by arbitrary and unnecessary limitations. We are also unable to break out of certain perspectives, whether through habit, emotional investment, or reinforcement.

## Chapter 3. Rapid Idea Generation

"Just let your creative juices flow!" This is something you might often hear people advise you when they want you to unleash your inner Artist and generate as many ideas as possible, to which you probably internally replied, "Um, okay, how?" You'll rarely get to hear anyone tell you just how this could be accomplished. It just ends up feeling like someone is encouraging you to be taller or have different colored eyes.

Are you supposed to just sit in a room and generate novel thoughts from nothing? Are you supposed to watch Stanley Kubrick movies to gain inspiration? What about meditating with a pen and paper nearby? As you might recall from the previous chapter, creative ideas can't always be had just by waiting for inspiration or a flash of genius. Rather, creativity is stimulated by hard work, thinking outside the box, and unconventional thinking.

Creativity is less like waiting for the rain of inspiration to fall from the heavens and more like constructing a pipeline from a water source, or maybe digging up your own well until water seeps from underground to fill it up. To do so, you'll need to have the proper tools and techniques—and these are what we'll be discussing for the next few chapters. Of course, this relates back to one of the building blocks from the prior chapter: that inspiration is a myth, and creativity is *work*.

You'll be equipped with the thinking tools you need to dig up your own well of ideas. After all, ideas are what you use to create whatever you want, no matter what field or discipline you're in. To seek to be creative is to seek ideas and to pursue new ways of looking at things. Whether what you're facing is a creative task, a work problem, or a personal dilemma, you'll need to generate ideas to tackle it, and the following chapters will teach you how to do so efficiently. In truth, this and the next chapter describe what people are actually seeking when they desire creativity.

But before discovering what tools would help you rapidly move forward in idea generation, it's important to first be aware of the common hindrances to generating those ideas. It would be harder to move forward with anything if you keep running up against the same wall, and you don't even know that it's your very own habits that keep leading you to it. So what might be those walls that could hold you back from generating great ideas?

Copywriter Dean Rieck says that one barrier to creativity is attempting to create while evaluating at the same time. Generating ideas and judging the soundness of those ideas require two different types of thinking that are incompatible with each other. Trying to do both at the same time is like trying to be the Artist and the Judge simultaneously—you can't fully become the prolific Artist generating great ideas, when you're also trying to be the stern Judge critiquing each idea even before it has a chance to fully emerge.

Secondly, another barrier is what Rieck calls "the expert syndrome." Every discipline already has gurus who tell you they've "been there, done that" and that if they've never done it themselves, then you can't either. Listen to and consider what they say, but don't follow them blindly either. Dare to try something that's never been done, even by experts—that's what innovation is all about, after all. Staying within a set of rules imposed on you by someone else is essentially putting your creativity in chains. For the most part, rules are arbitrarily set by someone who is not in your unique situation.

Third, fear of failure is also a major hindrance to creativity. To fear failure is also to fear trying, and when you don't try, you can never succeed. So as Rieck says, in trying so hard to avoid failure, you'll end up avoiding success too. The path to both failure and success starts in exactly the same way, and they might even be the same 99 percent of the way through, only diverging slightly at the end. You never know until you start.

Finally, false limits could trap you in a headspace that also stifles creativity. False limits are boundaries you've often drawn yourself and serve to keep you only to what's familiar and comfortable. But comfort is the enemy of creativity. To be creative is to go beyond what's familiar and comfortable and onto surprising and sometimes even bizarre new connections found only outside of your comfort zone. For example, if everyone limited themselves to the idea that printers could only print two-dimensional surfaces, then the world would not know the 3D plastic and metal printers of today.

In trying to generate ideas, be vigilant against those barriers to creativity. Let the Artist in you run free first without being stifled by the Judge or by gurus who try to tell you what's possible and what's not. Don't be afraid of making mistakes, failing, or coloring outside the lines. When you know how to avoid such traps to creativity, you can then make better use of the following tactics to help you generate ideas more rapidly.

Finally, it's helpful to understand that there are certain primary roles for you to play in your quest for creativity. These four roles are the *Explorer, Artist, Judge, and Warrior, and* they were described by Roger von Oech. However, we are really only concerned with the first two.

**Explorer**. The Explorer asks, "What's out there, and is it helpful?" The Explorer is intensely curious and perpetually in search of interesting and relevant ideas. It gathers gems from different fields of knowledge, poking around in both familiar and unfamiliar areas to find useful information. Remember how creativity is the art of finding new ways to see and use what's already there? Well, it's the Explorer's job to first figure out what's actually there. What is the current landscape, and where do the boundaries (arbitrary or not) appear to be? What lies beyond them?

The Explorer gathers raw materials for the creative project, including facts, opinions, feelings, and experiences. It refuses to be limited to just popular opinion or expert advice and instead seeks fresh perspectives. As the Explorer, gather everything, put it in one place, and then move on to the next role of the Artist.

***Artist.*** The Artists asks, "What do these things make me think of?" The Artist is full of ideas on what to do with the raw materials the Explorer has collected. The Explorer gathered the dots, and now the Artist works on connecting those dots in new and meaningful ways. The Artist is what people typically refer to when they say "creative." It looks at all the materials available and figures out a way to combine them in novel and sometimes out-of-this-world ways. The Artist takes raw materials and then becomes "inspired" by them.

Having a playful and daring streak, the Artist isn't inhibited by conventions as it experiments with combinations, reimagines concepts, and redefines trends. For example, as the Artist, you would pull together ideas from nutrition, marketing, and even animated characters to get children to choose and enjoy healthier food. The Artist in you might imagine how to use that passionate, animated rat chef Ratatouille to help get kids to eat nutritious, delectable meals. The Artist is often the one responsible for rapid idea generation.

***Judge***. The Judge is a practical and realistic character that performs the necessary reality check for the creative endeavor. While the Artist may be more of a free spirit, the Judge is more levelheaded and ensures that musings end up being actual creations. It analyzes each idea for feasibility, questioning assumptions and drawing counterarguments to bring out what's truly worthwhile.

***Warrior***. The Warrior fights to materialize and sell ideas in the real world. It's one thing to think creatively and another to fight for those thoughts to be turned into reality and be recognized as worthwhile.

Among these four roles, the Artist is what we're most concerned with developing when it comes to upgrading our creative selves. Creativity is mainly about the ability to generate ideas on how to connect the dots in new ways, and this is precisely the Artist's job.

These tactics will teach you practical and effective tools for stimulating your mind to think outside the box and develop new perspectives so you can get more creative in any aspect of your life. The first tactic is something that might sound ridiculous at the outset, but possesses a method to the madness.

**Tactic 1: 100 Ideas List**

Think back to a time when you tried to come up with ideas for a creative assignment or a problem needing a creative solution. Chances are you thought up or jotted down a few ideas, then stopped when you just couldn't think of any more. How many ideas did you manage to come up with before stopping? Five, ten, or maybe twenty at most? You'll notice that they were all somewhat related to each other and in the same vein of thought or approach. Then, when you hit the first mental drought, you stopped.

Trying to generate ideas takes up mental energy, so when people find that they have already listed down several, they think that's enough because they start to feel too tired and drained of mental energy to go any further. However, experiencing that initial feeling of tiredness doesn't mean that you've already generated all the ideas that you can.

If anything, it means that you've only finished listing down all the obvious answers and familiar things you know—you're done picking just all the low-hanging fruit, so to speak. To get to the more precious bounty higher up in the tree, you'll need to do some more climbing up—that is, make an effort to change the way you think and see things in order to generate even more creative ideas.

So to push you to go beyond the low-hanging fruit and get to as many "fruits of creativity" as you can, challenge yourself to make a list of a hundred ideas. No matter what it is you're trying to come up with ideas for—what to paint, the plot of your next novel, ways to recycle paper, how to increase customer satisfaction—resolve to list down a hundred ideas about it. Just write down one idea after another. Don't worry about editing the list and simply keep going until you reach one hundred.

Now here's the method to the madness: the purpose of this tactic is to propel your creative process by brute force, pushing you beyond your usual go-to responses and compelling you to drastically switch the direction of your thinking at several points in order to complete the hundred-ideas requirement. Where the first ten ideas sprung from the same approach or perspective, you'll have to find different themes or methods for the next ten. You'll find that when you've squeezed all the juice out of a particular lemon, you'll be forced to find other lemons and squeeze all the juice out of them, too. This gets you beyond the low-hanging fruit and into actual zones of creativity.

Say that for a charity function, or maybe a party, you're trying to think of ways you can serve hot home-cooked food to people at another site two hours away by car. Initially, you might think of the following methods to keep the food hot while in transit:

1. Use containers with airtight lids
2. Wrap the food containers in thick cloth

3. Use insulated carrier bags
4. Place the food in a hot water bath
5. Cover the food completely with aluminum foil wrap
6. Use heated bricks to line your food bucket

As you may notice, all of the above ideas are directed toward keeping food hot by surrounding it with material that's either hot or keeps heat from escaping. That first set of ideas was all about using containers and other methods that keep hot food hot. What do you do once you've exhausted all ideas in that direction? Shift to a different perspective. Thus far you've worked under the assumption that there's no way for you to reheat or prepare the food on-site. But what if you lift away that limit? Then you might come up with the following ideas to heat or even cook food on-site:

7. Bring your own portable electric stove
8. Bring a microwave
9. Bring a grill and coal
10. Bring an electric kettle and use it to make a hot water bath
11. Bring wood and a fire-starting kit

12. Set up the food in serving trays with a continuous heat source underneath
13. Bring a droplight that can heat the food placed below it
14. See if you can have access to reheating or other kitchen equipment on-site (e.g., homes or establishments that may lend their kitchens to you)

Then, when you run out of ideas in this particular direction, you again need to shift your perspective to generate more ideas. Aside from using heat-preserving containers or reheating/prepping food on-site yourself, what else might you be able to do to accomplish your task? With that, you might come up with the following ideas:

15. Look for alternative routes that will significantly shorten travel time by car
16. Find other modes of transportation that might shorten travel time
17. Rent a specialized delivery service from a caterer near you
18. Order food from restaurants or caterers nearer the site
19. Contract local home cooks at the site to do the cooking

20. Transport the people you intend to serve the food to closer to you

As you can see, by forcing yourself to come up with more and more ideas to fill one hundred empty slots, the scope of your thinking will also widen. From just considering how precooked food may be kept hot by the kind of containers you use to transport it, your thinking can evolve to include ideas from an entirely new perspective, such as bringing the people closer to you instead of you needing to deliver the food to them. Perhaps another way to look at this is not to have a quota of one hundred ideas, but instead a quota of multiple approaches, angles, perspectives, and veins of thought.

Of course, not each of the ideas you put in the list would be completely practical, but remember, you're not allowed to evaluate how good each idea is while you're generating them one after another. Your only task is to complete the hundred ideas list, no matter how weird or impractical or unsuitable your ideas might be. If out of those hundred, only one is actually good, then you still win—you got to a point where you came up with an idea that works, and most of the time that's all you need to get the job done.

## Tactic 2: Forced Randomization

How many times have you encountered a truly astonishing new idea, story or creation and thought, "Wow, I would never have imagined putting those two things together"? The random can be understood as a well of possibility—and systematic randomization is a powerful way to generate new, unexpected, deeply creative ideas from this well.

You may have heard about techniques such as free thinking, free writing, free association—all strategies that attempt to unhook the mind from what it already knows, take it out of its usual ruts and invite it to run loosely through concepts that might not ordinarily find themselves in one another's company. Being deliberately and systematically random is a way to access and generate new ideas and think far outside of the box. But how exactly do you do this?

Creativity has a lot to do with tapping the resources that are already available around you—be it objects, places, or people, among others—and discovering gems that may be hidden in them. To do so, you'll need to compel yourself to consider the common in unusual ways and combine ideas in a random fashion to give you the most chances of uncovering interesting connections. This is why another way you can generate ideas quickly is by forcing yourself to sample varying things and ideas, as well as experiment with connections randomly. There are a number of techniques you can use.

***Play shiritori***. This technique utilizes the Japanese game of *shiritori* to get your ideas flowing. *Shiritori* is a game where you start with a word, then think of another word that begins with the last letter of that first word—and on and on it goes. Say you're trying to conceptualize the theme of your next office party. If you start with the word "retro," next come up with another word that starts with an "O," such as "opera." To boost your brainstorming, simultaneously come up with ideas while you think up the next word. For instance, consider how "opera" may be applied to an office party. Would you consider having a party inspired by the feel of a 17th-century opera house, complete with a musical ensemble playing classical music and partygoers in theater play costumes?

Note the thoughts associated with that second word, then keep going with the *shiritori* technique by next coming up with another word that starts with the letter "A" (the last letter of the word "opera"). Again, think up how that word may apply as a party theme. Don't be critical of each idea as it occurs; just let the words flow one after another and allow them to inspire you. Keep this up until you have generated a good number of ideas, then later evaluate each idea to figure out the best one.

***Try random input***. Spark a fresh flow of ideas in your mind by opening a book to a random page, selecting a random word from a dictionary, or reading a random article on Wikipedia. If, for example, you opened the dictionary and your finger landed on the word "exhibit," think of how that word may apply as a party theme. How about having a party featuring an art exhibit of works relevant to your company or your employees' preferences? That's just one application of a random word, and you may consider many more applications of the same word, or select another random word as a starting point for another slew of ideas.

***Use the alphabet.*** Think of ideas beginning with each letter of the alphabet, and by the end of this exercise, you'd have twenty-six new ideas. In trying to come up with your party theme, for instance, you may run down the alphabet and churn out ideas for each letter: Aztec, Bohemian, countries, dinosaurs, elements, fantasy, Greek, heroes, India, jewels… and the list goes on.

***Combine random objects.*** Pick out two random objects and force a connection between them. Say you see a colleague's pearl earrings and take "pearl" as the first object. Then you look out the window and see a poster of a punk rock concert. How might you connect these two to create an interesting party idea? Maybe you can consider a "concert under the sea" theme. How about when you try to connect "photo album" and "cars"? Forcing a relationship between them, you may think of the photo album as representing memories throughout the years and cars as a method of traveling, leading you to a "journey through memories" party theme.

As you can see, this technique can help you directly by facilitating the flow of creative ideas applicable to your current task. Moreover, it can help you indirectly by training your mind to make random connections and thus exercise your creative brain muscles and boost your creativity in general. You'll practice spotting similarities and differences and constructing a logical story involving two unrelated elements. Sounds creative to me.

***Use Harvey cards.*** Harvey cards are a set of cards you can use to generate ideas. They contain cues, instructions, or questions you can ask yourself to stimulate creative thinking, such as "Animate – How can you imbue your subject with human qualities?" and "Symbolize – Convert your subject into a symbol." Write or print them out with one cue per card, shuffle them, and randomly pick one card from the deck. Brainstorm how you can apply the principle of that card to your creative task. Repeat this process over with the other cards and avoid skipping cards even if you find them hard.

Aside from these two, other cues you may have in your Harvey cards include the following:

- *Contradict* (reverse the original function of your subject)
- *Superimpose* (overlap dissimilar images or ideas with one another)
- *Transfer* (relocate your subject to a new situation or environment)
- *Add* (expand or supplement your subject)
- *Substitute* (replace an image or idea with another)
- *Distort* (twist the shape or meaning of your subject)
- *Transform* (put your subject in a state of change, akin to a caterpillar-cocoon-butterfly transformation)
- *Sympathize* (put yourself in your subject's shoes)
- *Analogize* (identify similarities between dissimilar things)
- *Subtract* (remove an element or break a rule)
- *Isolate* (disassemble and use only parts of something)

- *Disguise* (hide or camouflage your subject)
- *Change size* (enlarge or reduce your subject or alter proportions)
- *Repeat* (duplicate a shape, color, or idea)
- *Mythologize* (build a myth involving your subject)
- *Fantasize* (think of your subject in surreal, outrageous, or bizarre ways)
- *Combine* (merge or connect things)
- *Parody* (ridicule or make fun of your subject)

This technique forces you to consider the subject of your creative task in a myriad of different ways, thus stretching your mind to think of possibilities you may never have considered before. Say you're thinking of ways to make a bookshelf more interesting. Using the cue card "Animate," imbue the bookshelf with human qualities, such as having arms and hands to "hold" the books. Or if you pick out the card "Symbolize," consider symbolisms related to the bookshelf, such as "doors to learning" or "vessels of knowledge." Use these symbolisms to reimagine the bookshelf, possibly reconstructing it to incorporate a doorway or evoke the look of a barrel.

Finally, give ***clustering*** a try. As you well know, people can get stuck in cognitive ruts, failing to explore an idea fully or looking at possible connections to other ideas they haven't taken the time to appreciate. Clustering is like loosening, dissecting and unravelling old ideas to make way for new ones. Much like Austrian psychologist Sigmund Freud would have asked you to lie back and randomly say whatever comes into your mind in therapy, the clustering technique is all about associations—and the juiciest ones are often hidden or unconscious.

The idea is to let go of linear thinking, and surprise yourself. Draw links. Scramble or invert your preconceived ideas or assumptions. Expand your thinking to include *feeling* and non-verbal information like sounds, images, intuitions, smells, tastes, or weird mixes of all of these.

The best way to understand the process is through concrete example. Perhaps I am "brainstorming" from scratch an idea for an ad campaign for a beauty product. I start quite randomly with the word "water." I relax and let my mind wander to whatever it wants to, and notice I think of other words: cool, blue, quiet, pure. My mind is drawn to *pure*. I let it make its own leaps and jumps, not stopping to question whether my associations make sense. I might see the image of an angel, smell a bar of soap, imagine the face of Grace Kelly, or hear the sound of a crisp, clear-sounding bell. I see a color palette of blue and white.

Perhaps I keep track of these associations and connections on paper, and they may well look like a sprawling mind map, with the central idea branching off into other related ideas. Perhaps I decide to divide the *angelic* branch and explore this idea further, splitting it off into two ideas—beautiful, and childlike. Of course, in the example, these particular associations are very personal and unique to the person having them, and it's important not to censor them as they emerge.

I keep going, pressing further out. I don't question that the first thought that pops into my mind when I dwell on "childlike" is "round." I draw smooth circles and ovals on my mind map to cement this association. Somehow, my unconscious mind is making connections to something womblike, spherical, full, even amoeba-like. Quite a far-cry from my original "water" idea!

You'll notice that each node or jump is an indiscriminate mix of mood, thought, image or sensation. There are no rules, except perhaps to note down what pops into your head quickly before you have time to second-guess yourself. The strength of this process is the almost infinite potential paths it opens up to explore. Any one of these ideas could split and sprawl out into an entirely new direction. With just a little time, a single idea or thought can be exploded and fractionated into millions of tiny offshoots.

I could use this example to generate the beginnings of a print ad for a new face wash—can you picture an amorphous, silvery-blue image of a beautiful round, angelic face hovering over a clear pool of water? This image itself could serve as a springboard for a copywriting team to devise just the right words to conjure al the moods and images uncovered in the clustering exercise. But there are other ways to use this freeform idea-generating technique. It's also great for shaking loose writer's block, for generating novel solutions whenever you feel stuck with a problem, or even for engaging more deeply with material you're trying to understand and learn. Finally, clustering is a great way to "brain dump" and process what's in your heart and mind, showing that creativity, self-knowledge and our innermost experiences are all connected.

## Tactic 3: Thinking More "Plainly"

The third tactic is to attempt to strip away meaning and get back to the basics. When we think of creativity, we often conjure visions of elaborate and detailed masterpieces that are one of a kind. But while these masterpieces are indeed products of creativity, we typically make the mistake of thinking that the process of creating them also required detailed and elaborate thought. We fail to recognize that while the product may look intricate and complex, the process that created it may have first required simplicity in thinking. Here's another tactic that creatives know how to use well: if you want to generate ideas rapidly, you have to learn how to think more plainly.

Thinking more plainly means zooming out and having a looser perspective on things. It's being able to grasp the gist of the problem rather than getting stuck on its minute details. This type of thinking can be practiced by replacing problem-specific verbs with generic ones when stating the problem. For instance, don't ask, "How could I *drive* something over a long distance?" Instead, think, "How could I *move* something over a long distance?"

Moving covers not just driving but also flying, swimming, sliding, throwing, crawling into a catapult, and more. Using the looser, more generic verb "move" opens up more possibilities because it removes the restrictions of the specific verb "drive." A study by Clement and colleagues demonstrated how such a technique can dramatically improve performance in tasks requiring analogical thinking. They found that when problems were described in more generic terms, the participants' performance improved by over 100 percent in some tasks.

So if you're tackling a creative task or problem, write it down and highlight or circle the verbs and keywords you used. Then consider if there's a more general umbrella term those words belong under and opt to use that term instead. With your task now phrased in a more generic way, rethink the possibilities considering this new formulation.

Thinking more plainly encourages rapid idea generation because by considering matters in more universal terms you also widen your view of what's possible. The wider your playground, the more areas you have for exploration and discovery. One of the biggest hindrances to idea generation is when you limit your thinking to a small area only, which is exactly what happens when you phrase the task in specific terms instead of general ones. You start to get tunnel vision and fail to see the variables and givens actually present in the situation. Such a perspective severely limits your options and thus also hinders you from generating ideas and creative solutions for your problem.

In the same way, seeing only the specific, common uses of things is another major obstacle to creativity. Known as "functional fixedness," this creativity-blocker surfaces when you have everything you need to solve the problem, but you can't do it because you see only the usual or traditional function of the objects you have. You get stuck (i.e., "fixed") on that sole specific function of the object, so you're inhibited from thinking of any more creative uses for it to help you in your current situation.

Psychologist Tom McCaffrey demonstrates this concept by setting the two-rings problem, which challenges participants to fasten together two heavy steel rings with only the following: a two-inch steel cube, a long candle, and a match. He adds the condition that melted wax would not be strong enough to secure the rings together.

The solution to the problem requires an escape from functional fixedness. You would first need to get past the view of the candle's usual function and recognize that its wick is not just for burning but is also a piece of string you can use to fasten things together. If you allowed yourself to fixate on the common, specific function of a candle, then you would be inhibited from using it to solve your problem.

Thus, the key to generating solutions is to escape the trap of functional fixedness by thinking of objects in more generic terms. To this end, McCaffrey developed the *generic parts technique*. This technique involves first breaking things down into their component parts with more generic descriptions (e.g., a candle has a wick, which qualifies as a string in general), then asking yourself how you can use that component to solve the problem (e.g., how having a string can help you out). So again, it's by thinking more plainly in such generic descriptions that you move toward producing effective solutions and creative ideas.

So the next time you want to generate more creative ideas, think in simpler, more general, and universal terms. For instance, instead of wondering how you would *paint* your store walls in an interesting way, consider how you would *make* those walls interesting. The more general term "make" opens up more possibilities for your creativity to run wild, going beyond just brushing paint onto a wall and instead leading you to experiment with other materials, textures, and techniques to make that wall truly one of a kind.

## Tactic 4: Idea Box

Finally, as many masters of creativity know, creativity is less about making new ideas from scratch and more about forging new connections among already existing ideas, materials, and techniques. This tactic helps you do exactly the latter, in an organized and systematic way, so that you don't miss any opportunity to spot an interesting connection, wherever it may arise. Called the idea box, this technique involves constructing a grid that helps you have a clear picture of the possibilities and potential areas of innovation no matter what your creative project may be.

To construct your own idea box, first enumerate the essential parameters of the product or service you want to generate ideas on. This builds on other concepts for idea generation, notably combination and methodical lists. For example, you're trying to invent a new home item. Some parameters you may include are location, shape, material, and purpose. Write these parameters at the topmost row of your grid, like so:

|   | Location | Shape | Material | Purpose |
|---|----------|-------|----------|---------|
| 1 |          |       |          |         |
| 2 |          |       |          |         |
| 3 |          |       |          |         |
| 4 |          |       |          |         |

Next, list down the different variations or options under each parameter. For the parameter location, for instance, you may write down living room, kitchen, bedroom, and bathroom. In the same way, list different variations of each parameter under their respective columns:

|   | Location | Shape | Material | Purpose |
|---|---|---|---|---|
| 1 | Living room | Cube | Wood | Storage |
| 2 | Kitchen | Round | Metal | Decoration |
| 3 | Bedroom | Elongated | Plastic | Organization |
| 4 | Bathroom | Irregular | Glass | Functional tool |

After you've completely filled out your grid, now it's time to generate those ideas! Pick out one option per parameter and conceptualize how they might be *combined* to create your new home item. For example, combine bathroom (location), irregular (shape), glass (material), and organization (purpose).

Merge these four elements in your mind and let your creativity flow. You want something that's made of glass, irregularly shaped, and used to organize things in the bathroom. Is there a vision forming in your head? What object are you imagining? Maybe you begin to visualize an interesting star-shaped glass cupboard you can affix to the wall, with each of the star's spikes holding a different type of bath item, toiletries, or other supplies. This is just one possible combination you can have with the four-by-four idea box above—and using such a grid, you have a total of 254 potential ideas at your fingertips.

Idea boxes are typically four-by-four grids, such as the example above, or often have six-by-six dimensions. For your own idea box, you may have more parameters and options as you see fit, with each addition yielding exponentially more ideas and solutions. As you randomly combine the different variations of your parameters, you stimulate your mind to use even combinations you've never considered before. The idea box is a way to generate loads of ideas in an organized and systematic manner. So challenge yourself to use all the variations in your box, such that you force your thinking beyond the comfortable and the obvious in order to obtain truly unique and innovative outcomes. Also remember to avoid evaluating and critiquing your ideas at this stage; just let them flow freely and in all possible directions.

So there you have it—a whole bag of tools that would help you formulate fresh ideas more rapidly and effectively. Whether you strive to list a hundred ideas, opt for forced randomization, try to think more plainly in generic terms, or use the idea box, you'll be sure to produce at least a gem or two you'll find useful in crafting that creative output or solution.

Remember, too, that as you use any of those tools, you need to be mindful of the barriers that might hinder your creativity. Avoid judging ideas while in the process of generating them, don't be quick to blindly believe expert opinion, remember that making mistakes is part of the creative process, and dare to go beyond the comfortable and the familiar. Breaking free of what's holding you back from creating, combined with using the right tools for idea generation, leads you to the fullest use of your creative potentials.

Takeaways:

- Ideas are a valuable resource that can determine your fate, whether it's your career or how comfortable you are on your couch. While we can utilize some of the creativity building blocks, there are specific techniques to generate more ideas in less time. Generating ideas out of thin air is difficult, so it always helps to have methods to organize the fog that is your brain.
- First, shoot for a hundred ideas. This sounds like madness, but there is a method to the madness. Often, ideas are difficult because we are stuck along one line of thought. You're in your box. Trying for one hundred forces you to think differently and abandon lines of thought. It pushes you into a zone of absurdity and "why not?" and that's more or less where thinking outside the box begins.
- Second, make friends with randomization. This can take the form of

playing *shiritori*, using the alphabet, forcing relationships between random objects, random input, creating and using Harvey cards, and giving clustering (similar to mind maps) a shot.
- Third, try to let go of the emotions and attachments you place on things and think more plainly. Consider problems more generally as opposed to specifically, and try to get away from the negative effects of functional fixedness.
- Finally, systematically create combinations with an idea box.

# Chapter 4. Rapid Idea Generation Part 2

If the prior chapter didn't contain enough ideas for rapid idea generation, I'm pleased to be able to bring you another entire chapter! For most of us, this is truly what we're seeking when we think of creativity—practical tactics for everyday insights. Not all of us want to live a life like the polymathic da Vinci or dedicate ourselves to the pursuit of the new and novel, but that doesn't mean we can't employ creativity to make our everyday world a little bit better.

So without further ado, here are three more wide-ranging techniques to generate more ideas. They are slightly more process- or perspective-driven than the previous chapter's techniques. Remember, use what works for you, and discard that which does not resonate. The *idea* is to give you more *ideas* for generating *ideas*.

## Tactic 5: Wear Six Hats

This is a useful concept from Edward de Bono, researcher and author known for his thoughts on thinking. Now, we've all heard the term that you must wear more than one hat, and as you might have guessed, this method requires looking at a problem or decision from six separate perspectives by wearing six different hats. This is probably five more perspectives than you're used to, which injects a certain amount of creativity into your mind. It's not that the hats here are creative by themselves, but the combination of the six of them can drastically change your perception to be more creative and open.

Along with the hats themselves, an avatar that embodies the main purpose of each hat will make matters much clearer. It's like you are making a decision by committee, but all the roles are played by you. This allows you to uncover a wide range of perspectives outside of your own, and we know how important it is to gather sources at this point. Different patterns of thought give rise to different ideas, as well as a combination of ideas.

The colors of the six hats are white, red, black, yellow, green, and blue. The colors are fairly inconsequential, and it's probably easier if you categorize them by the avatar. I'll go into each of them in depth.

*"Tell me more. What does this mean, and where did you get that information?"*

The white hat is Sherlock Holmes, of course. This is the thinking and analytical hat. You are trying to gather as much information as possible by whatever means possible. Be observant and act like an information sponge. While you're at it, analyze your information and determine the gaps you have and what you can deduce from your current knowledge. Dig deep, fill in the information gaps, and try to gather an understanding of what you really have in front of you.

You want to absorb as much of the available information as you can while also determining what you are missing to make a more informed and suitable decision. The white hat is also where you should be resourceful about learning. As we discussed earlier, lack of information is one of the worst detriments to your decisions.

Make sure you are armed with information, seek multiple perspectives and don't let yourself be influenced by bias. You want an objective view of the entire landscape. Get out your magnifying glass and start sleuthing, Detective Holmes.

*"And how does that make you feel? Why is that?"*

The red hat is Sigmund Freud, the psychotherapist. This is your emotion hat. You are trying to determine how you feel about something and what your gut tells you. Those are not always the same emotions. Combined with the information you collected as Sherlock Holmes, this will already give you a more complete picture than you are used to.

You are asking how you feel about your options and why. Beyond the objective level, decisions affect us on an emotional level. You must account for that—happiness and unhappiness. Ask yourself what you find yourself leaning toward or avoiding and why that might be. You can also attempt to predict how others might react emotionally.

Your actions might have consequences beyond your current understanding, and how people will feel is often different from how you think they will feel. What are the origins of your emotions toward each option, and are they reasonable or even relevant, for that matter? Often, our emotions aren't in the open, so when you can understand them better, you will understand your options better as well.

*"I don't know. I have my doubts. What about X? Will Y really happen that way?"*

The black hat is Eeyore, the morose donkey from *Winnie the Pooh*. If you don't know who that is, you can imagine the black hat to be the ultimate depressed pessimist that never believes anything will work out. Indeed, the purpose of the black hat is to attempt to poke holes in everything and to try to account for everything that can go wrong. They are skeptics who always look on the darker side of life.

They believe in *Murphy's law*: everything that can go wrong *will* go wrong. This is a hat most people never wear because they are afraid to look at their decisions or reasoning from a critical point of view. On some level, it probably indicates recognition that their views fall apart under deeper scrutiny, but that is exactly why it's so important to wear the black hat.

This viewpoint is essentially planning for failure and the worst-case scenario. Planning for success is easy and instantaneous, but what happens when things don't work out and you have to put out fires? How would you prepare differently if you thought there was a high probability of failure?

You change your approach, look for alternatives, and create contingency plans to account for everything. This is the type of analysis that leads to better planning and decisions because you can objectively take into account what is good and what is not.

Wearing your black hat makes your plans tougher and stronger over the long haul, though it can be exhausting to continually reject positivity and hopefulness—which is why we have alternative hats to turn to as well.

*"It's going to be so great when this all comes together. Just imagine how you'll feel."*

The yellow hat is the cheerleader. It is the opposite of the black hat—you are now thinking positively and optimistically. This is a motivating hat that allows you to feel good about your decision and the value of putting all the work into it. This is where you turn dark clouds into a silver lining.

It also allows you to project into the future and imagine the opportunities that come along with it. If this decision goes well, what else will follow? Where do optimistic projections place you, and what is necessary for you to reach them?

Belief in yourself is still one of the concepts that fuels achievement and motivation, so it's important to be balanced with pessimism and nitpicking flaws.

*"Call me crazy, but what if we completely change X and try Y?"*

The green hat is Pablo Picasso, the famous artist. This hat is for creativity. When you wear this hat, you want to think outside the box and come up with creative perspectives, angles, and solutions to whatever you are facing. It can be as simple as pretending that your current leading option is unavailable and having to figure out what you can do instead. You must deviate from the current options and discover other ways of solving your problem.

Brainstorming is the name of the game here. No judgment or criticism is allowed when you are wearing this hat because you want to generate as many ideas as possible. You can always curate them later, but the more solutions you can think of, no matter how zany or ineffective, there will always be something you can learn or apply from them.

This is also a hat of open-mindedness and not being stuck in one track of thinking, which can be dangerous if you refuse to alter your course in the face of hardships.

*"Now, now, children. Everyone will have their turn to be heard."*

The blue hat is Henry Ford, founder of Ford Motor Company and inventor of the modern assembly line. The blue hat is all about coordinating and creating a system to integrate all the information you obtained from the other hats. You can also look at this hat as the CEO: you are in charge of making things happen and putting things in place, though not necessarily creating anything by yourself.

You are in charge of weighing how heavily each hat should be considered and what factors you must take into account when integrating the information. The CEO knows the context the best, so the input from each different hat is synthesized and weighed based on personal priorities and the situation at hand. You are the ultimate decider.

These six perspectives should get your mind jumping at the number of perspectives that you aren't using. For instance, what would your role model do? Or how might da Vinci himself think about something? How would someone that you admire, with a distinct combination of positive traits, approach what you are looking at? For that matter, what about a distinct combination of *negative* traits?

What kind of ideas would spring from their head? Batman might generate morbid, brutal ideas, but Wonder Woman might be completely different.

Shifting your perspective is an important aspect of the problem-solving process, especially when you're faced with a complex problem for which traditional views and thinking styles just don't cut it anymore. When you need creative solutions for highly challenging or unconventional scenarios, you can count on several perspective-shifting techniques to help you through.

### Tactic 6: Use Intentional Constraints

When it comes to creativity, it's common for people to equate it with the idea of abundance—an abundance of materials, time, and other resources is easily seen as an effective prompter of fresh ideas and innovative solutions. An artist given a wealth of art supplies and provisions must be in wonderland, possessing the highest chances of turning out a uniquely crafted masterpiece. That's often what we want, even in this book!

A chef provided with a huge variety of the best ingredients is imagined as having everything needed to churn out an inspired dish. The prevalent idea is that the more that is loaded into the creative's arsenal, the better the output will be. The more ideas and freedom, the better your chance to generate a solution to your problems.

But is that the best method to solve problems or the best way to spur the flow of fresh ideas and solutions? There is a big difference between the two.

Compared to piling on the resources and broadening options, putting up constraints and limiting resources appear to spark creativity better. Psychologist and creativity expert Patricia Stokes of Columbia University has seen such a principle at work in an experiment she conducted in 1993. Her study demonstrated how rodents constrained to press a bar using only their right paws resulted in those rodents devising more creative ways of pressing the bar compared to rodents that were free to use all their limbs.

This is what's known as "little 'c' creativity," a form of creativity aimed at addressing practical problems rather than yielding artistic output. And with the number and complexity of emerging 21st-century problems needing resourceful solutions in the face of scarcity, little "c" creativity may be the next big thing.

To test how people's creative use of resources may be influenced by thinking about scarcity or abundance, Ravi Mehta and Meng Zhu conducted a study using "the bubble wrap test" in 2015. They predicted that thinking about scarcity would boost people's capacity to use resources in unconventional ways.

To test that prediction, Mehta and Zhu randomly divided sixty undergrads into two groups. One group was instructed to write an essay about growing up with scarce resources, while the other group was to write about growing up with abundant resources. Both groups were then tasked to come up with a solution for a real problem their university faced: how to put to good use 250 bubble wrap sheets that were byproducts of a recent move of their computer lab.

After drafting a proposal for using the bubble wrap, the participants answered a survey on the different ways they tackled the problem. Twenty judges, blind to the participants' scarcity or abundance groupings, then scored the proposals in terms of the novelty of the ideas they put forward. The result? The scarcity group outperformed the abundance group in coming up with creative uses for the discarded bubble wrap.

The outcome of Mehta and Zhu's experiment reveals a counterintuitive but valuable point in the science of creativity—that sometimes, in order to force the mind to think outside the box, it is necessary to first make that box smaller and smaller, reining in the mind with fewer and fewer options so it has no choice but to reconstruct those options in unconventional ways. In other words, creativity appears to be less of an inborn personality trait and more of a response to environments and situations that compel the person to make the best use of whatever resource is available.

Say you're part of a marketing team tasked to come up with a print ad promoting your new product. If you were told you can fill an entire magazine with promotional information about your product, chances are you'll end up with something that may be highly informative and detailed, but overloaded with irrelevant details that will only bore prospective consumers instead of enticing them to buy your merchandise.

But if you deliberately constrain your ad to, say, a quarter of a page, your team is likely to generate vastly more interesting and eye-catching ad ideas. Precisely because you are given so little space to work with, you'll be forced to come up with the catchiest of taglines and the most striking of images to get your product noticed.

The following are more examples of how creative constraints can give rise to impressive solutions to the problems in front of you.

***Six-word memoirs***. Can an entire life be summed up in just six words? The book *Not Quite What I Was Planning* proves that the answer is yes—and with results ranging from the amusing to the profound, too. While traditional memoirs are often thick volumes filled with elaborate details and analysis of a life's beginnings, highlights, and struggles, *Not Quite What I Was Planning* breaks such a mold by showcasing a collection of six-word memoirs. Interesting examples include Stephen Colbert's "Well, I thought it was funny" and Linda Williamson's "Painful nerd kid, happy nerd adult." How about you? How would you sum up your life in six words?

As this creative venture shows, setting constraints on your projected output can lead to interesting results. Putting parameters on what you're allowed to produce—in this case, no more than six words to encapsulate an entire life—forces your brain to be more imaginative so as to meet the parameters without sacrificing the output's meaningfulness. Without such constraints on expected output, you'll be more likely to stick to just comfortable yet uninteresting solutions.

But introduce constraints, and you're on your way toward generating creative ideas you didn't imagine you had in you to produce.

***Career-ending injury***. They say every dark cloud has a silver lining. Artist Phil Hansen has proven that right, though he had to do more than just spot the silver lining. He had to suffer the dark cloud for years, then decide to create its silver lining. Phil had developed a specific pointillist style all throughout his years as an art student, but unfortunately met an injury that rendered him incapable of practicing the same technique ever again. Distraught and hopeless, he left the art world.

But though Phil tried to leave the artist in him behind, he later found that nothing could take the artist out of him. Three years later, he started to dabble in the arts again. But constrained by the repercussions of his injury, he had to develop a new art style that incorporated the shaky lines his quivering hands couldn't help but make. Embracing rather than resenting the constraints that his injury had put on him, Phil was thus led to craft unique and amazing art pieces only he could create—not despite his injury but because of it.

Phil's story illustrates how even limitations in personal capacity can serve as the trigger to produce more creative and unique outcomes. Not being able to do things in the same way you've always done them may be a hard pill to swallow, but in certain situations, that may be the very push you need to be more creative and discover new (often better) ways of doing things.

Another prime example of this is gypsy jazz guitarist Django Reinhardt. He was a seemingly normal guitarist until he was involved in a caravan accident involving a fire. Two of his fingers on his left hand, the important hand of a guitarist, were damaged so badly from burns that they were paralyzed and nearly amputated. Despite this, Reinhardt re-taught himself to play the guitar with 60 percent of a normal person's capacity (only three out of five fingers) and became renowned for his innovative playing.

If you find yourself constrained by your own incapacity to do things a certain way, take it as a challenge to change the way things have always been done. With this perspective, you'll be able to come up with ideas that may not just get things done, but revolutionize how they're accomplished.

***Copyright restrictions***. Poets are artists of their own kind, wordsmiths who gather their material from the seemingly endless constellation of words available to them at any given time. But what if even words are given to a poet in a limited fashion? Will that limit the poet's creativity or enhance it?

In the case of artist Austin Kleon, such constraint definitely boosts creativity. Known for his newspaper blackout poems, Kleon takes a newspaper page or column and then blacks out words using a marker until only his own poem or message is left visible. In addition to the limited words he has to work with, Kleon also has copyright restrictions to consider because he's using printed material written by someone else.

Needing to work in accordance with copyright law, Kleon is thus driven to creatively flesh out poems that either reverse, parody, or completely differ from the original message of the newspaper piece. Rather than limiting inspiration or originality, in Kleon's case, restrictions thus have the effect of spurring imagination and creativity.

As Kleon's inspired works illustrate, restricting the materials available for you to work with can get your creative juices flowing and lead you to produce remarkable output. While Kleon's materials were words, yours may be a host of different resources, including money, product supplies, tools, and other provisions. What Kleon's process proves is that limiting those resources doesn't necessarily have to equal to a decline in creativity.

On the contrary, by having no choice but to make use only of what's already available in short supply, you're forcing yourself to think outside the box. Precisely because you have such limited resources, it's your imagination that has to fill the gap by stretching itself to discover innovative solutions and ideas.

**Tactic 7: SCAMPER It**

Finally, one of the easiest ways to cultivate outside-the-box thinking and generate ideas is the SCAMPER method. Pioneered by Bob Eberle for precisely this purpose during brainstorming sessions, the SCAMPER method stands for seven techniques that help direct thinking toward innovative ideas and solutions: (S) substitute, (C) combine, (A) adapt, (M) minimize/magnify, (P) put to another use, (E) eliminate, and (R) reverse. Collectively, these techniques are based on the idea that you can come up with something new by simply modifying the old things already present around you.

The SCAMPER method works by forcing your mind to think in a new, specific flow, making it possible for you to reach novel solutions. Think of it as akin to opening a faucet that introduces water to seven pipes, and each of those pipes channels to a unique pot of earth. Each pot has the potential to bring forth a new growth once the seeds in it are watered. The SCAMPER method works in a similar way to nurture a new idea or solution out of you.

Note that the SCAMPER method doesn't require that you move in a sequential flow of steps. You may start with any of the thinking techniques it involves and jump among the different methods throughout your brainstorming or problem-solving session. Furthermore, it adapts the principle of *force-fitting*. This means that in order to come up with fresh solutions, you should be willing to integrate ideas, objects, or elements together—no matter how dissimilar, unrelated, or apparently illogical they seem to be.

Only by freeing your mind enough to connect things you never thought of linking before can you fully harness each of the following thinking techniques of the SCAMPER method. Indeed, this is a major element of SCAMPER because we are too often held back by our preconceptions and assumptions of what cannot be.

***Substitute***. This technique refers to replacing certain parts in the product, process, or service with another to solve a problem. To carry out this approach, first consider the situation or problem in light of having many elements—multiple materials, several steps in the process, different times or places at which the process can occur, various markets for the product or service, and the like. Then consider that each and every one of these elements may be replaced with an alternative.

Some questions that might help you get into this flow of thinking include the following: "Could a more cost-effective material replace the current one we're using without sacrificing product quality?" "What part of the process can be switched into a simpler alternative?" "In what other places can we offer our services?"

Let's say you're producing craft pieces that use a particular kind of glue as adhesive. However, you find that the glue you use easily dries out and clumps up even when stored properly, leading to wastage and more production costs. To solve this problem, consider brainstorming whether you might use a different adhesive to replace what you're currently using. Another example might be substituting local materials for imported ones, not only reducing costs on your end but also helping the local community in the process.

***Combine***. This technique suggests considering whether two products, ideas, or steps of a procedure may be combined to produce a single output or process that's better in some way. Two existing products could create something new if put together. Two old ideas could merge into a fresh, groundbreaking one if fused in the right way. Two stages of a process may be melded into one to create a more streamlined, efficient procedure.

Questions that can facilitate a line of thinking utilizing the combined technique include the following: "Can we put two or more elements together?" "Can we carry out two processes at the same time?" "Can we join forces with another company to improve our market strength?"

For instance, the combination of the spoon and fork has led to the innovation of the spork, a utensil now often packed within ready-to-eat noodle cups because of its cost-saving and convenient design. It solves the problem of having to manufacture two different utensils and effectively halves the cost of production.

***Adapt***. This technique intends to adjust something in order to enhance it. It solves problems by improving how things are typically done, with adjustments ranging from something small to something radical. It challenges you to think of ways that you can adjust what's already existing—be it a product, a process, or a manner of doing things—such that it solves a current problem and is better tailored to your needs.

Noticing that you have less energy than usual, for instance, you may think of solving the problem by making adjustments to your food choices, such as cutting back on empty calories and processed food. In the business world, this technique is also often utilized by brainstorming groups looking to enhance their product, service, or production process.

Some questions considered under this rubric include the following: "How can we regulate the existing process to save us more time?" "How can we tweak the existing product to sell better?" "How can we adjust the existing process to be more cost-effective?"

An example of an adaptation for a product is the development of mobile phone cases that have been imbued with shock absorbers or shockproof material. This clever tweak has obviously been developed in response to the common problem of accidentally dropping and consequently damaging fragile phone parts. In a similar vein, waterproofing mobile phone cases, wristwatches, and the like is another instance of adapting a product in order to improve it.

***Magnify or minimize.*** This technique involves either increasing or decreasing an element to trigger new ideas and solutions. Magnifying pertains to increasing something, such as by exaggerating a problem, putting more emphasis on an idea, making a product bigger or stronger, or doing a process more frequently.

On the other hand, minimizing entails decreasing something, such as by toning down a problem, deemphasizing an idea, reducing the size of a product, or carrying out a process less frequently. Thinking through certain elements in terms of either magnifying or minimizing them is bound to give you fresh insights as to the most and least significant parts of your problem, thus guiding you toward effective solutions.

Discussion questions that apply the magnify technique include the following: "How can you exaggerate or overstate the problem?" "What would be the outcome if you emphasized this feature?" "Will doing the process more frequently make a difference?" As for minimizing, challenge yourself to ponder on the following: "How will playing down this feature change the outcome?" "How can we condense this product?" "Will doing this step less frequently lead to better efficiency?"

Say that you've been assigned to transfer to a smaller office. You now have the problem of fitting your things into a more confined space. Using the magnify and minimize technique to resolve your dilemma, you can ask yourself questions as to which office components you would want to place more or less emphasis on. Are you going to place more emphasis on having space for receiving and meeting with clients, or for tech equipment or maybe for file storage?

Mulling over which aspect to magnify will help you pick out and arrange things in your new office in a way that best reflects your needs and values. As for using the minimize technique, consider which of your office stuff may be condensed together to fit a smaller floor area. For example, while previously you may have had separate tables for your computer and your printer, you may think of using a compact computer desk with a printer shelf instead.

***Put to another use***. This technique aims to figure out how an existing product or process may be used for a purpose other than what it's currently being used for. It stimulates a discussion on the myriad of other ways you might find a use for anything from raw materials to finished products to discarded waste. It's basically about finding a new purpose for old things.

Some questions that can facilitate this line of thinking include the following: "How else can this product be used?" "Can another part of the company use this material?" "Can we find a use for the bits we throw out?"

Consider how this would apply for stuff lying around in your own home. For instance, how would you address the problem of old newspapers just piling up in a corner? Using them to clean your windowpanes is a common solution, but how about finding other fresh ideas? By challenging yourself to think of more unconventional uses, you will magnify the way those old newspapers benefit you, from serving as trusty deodorizers for shoes to being raw materials for fun papier-mâché crafts.

***Eliminate.*** This technique refers to identifying the unnecessary elements of a project or process so that they can be eliminated and thus provide for an improved outcome. It considers how a procedure may be streamlined by dropping redundant steps or how the same output may be produced despite cutting resources. Whatever resource is freed up may then be used to enhance creativity and innovation.

Questions that make up this rubric include the following: "Is there any step we can remove without affecting the outcome?" "How would we carry out the same activity if we had half the resources?" "What would happen if we eliminated this part?"

One of the most useful applications of this technique is in the area of addressing financial problems in daily life. For example, you find that you're earning enough for your daily expenses but never get to put money aside for emergencies. Barring the option of gaining more income, the only thing left to do is subtract expenses so you can save for an emergency fund.

Using the eliminate technique, identify expenses you can cut—maybe pass up on buying that shiny new bag you don't really need, or opt for cheaper home-cooked meals instead of dining out. The money freed up from eliminating unnecessary expenses can then be your savings for use come rainy days.

***Reverse***. This technique suggests switching up the order of the process steps in order to find solutions and maximize innovative potentials. Also known as the rearrange technique, this line of thinking encourages interchanging elements or considering the process backward in order to stimulate a fresh take on the situation.

Some questions that apply the reverse technique include the following: "How would reversing the process change the outcome?" "What would happen if we did the procedure backward?" "Can we interchange one step with another?"

Say you're having trouble fulfilling your personal promise to exercise more. You've had it written in your schedule to spend thirty minutes exercising at the end of the day. But when it comes time for it, you always seem to have other, more urgent things to attend to or are too tired for it. Thus, you never get around to doing it consistently. To solve this problem, you may consider applying the reverse technique.

Check whether you may interchange your exercise time slot with another part of your day, such as making time for it first thing in the morning instead. By reversing the time you set for exercising, you may just find it easier to stick to the routine, as in the morning you're not yet drained or too beset by the day's activities.

The SCAMPER method is one of the easiest yet most effective strategies for finding solutions to problems and sparking creative thinking. Because it explores a process from seven different perspectives—substitute, combine, adapt, modify, put to another use, eliminate, and reverse—no stone is left unturned, and even unconventional solutions can be uncovered.

By forcing you to think in a specific, unique way, the SCAMPER method jolts your mind out of the regular pattern it's used to running and onto new roads worth exploring. And for every new path you explore, you generate new and varied ideas, creating a pool from which you can later draw the best solution to the problem at hand. Where you had one or two ways of looking at a problem, you now have seven additional approaches to apply.

## **<u>Tactic 8: Multitask (Yes, really)</u>**

Finally, let's now move on to something you might not ordinarily associate with creativity: multitasking.

We've all been told that multitasking is best avoided, since it slices up our concentration and weakens our ability to sustain attention for one task, dropping our productivity overall. But Professor David Burkas and researchers at the University of Sydney have now released a study showing that multitasking may actually be beneficial for creativity (with some large caveats). There were three groups of participants, and the first were given what's called an "alternative uses" task, which is essentially a test of creativity where you're given an object and asked to come up with as many different uses for that object as you can. The first group was given four uninterrupted minutes to do this task.

The second group was allowed to spend two uninterrupted minutes on finding creative uses for their object, but were then asked to switch and do a different creativity test (they were asked to come up with synonyms for given words). After completing this word task they returned to the object test and had a further two minutes to complete it.

The third group also had the two minutes on, two minutes off, but on their two minutes off, they completed a very undemanding and almost relaxing task of answering a short survey about themselves. Can you guess what results they found?

The first group generated the *fewest* creative ideas of all three groups (average 6.9 ideas), the second group was the next best (7.6 ideas when the break contained another creative task) and the third group performed best of all, with an average of 9.8 ideas when they stepped away from the task entirely. This result goes against much of what we've been taught about sustained attention and getting work done. It suggests that creativity benefits when we step away from a pursuit and return to it later. Similarly, merely shifting to a different creative task is a little better, but still not as powerful as completely "resting" your creativity muscle.

The researchers suggested that this happened because of the way we work on creative problems. If we get stuck in a rut, we can find ourselves going through the same concepts over and over, getting hung up on what we already know and further closing off any new avenues. Rather than actively coming up with something new, you simply cover the same ground over and over. When you take a break, however, you give your mind the opportunity to let go of these fixations, refresh itself and open up to new possibilities. You return to your work and see a solution all at once in so-called "eureka" moments.

What are we to make of all the research that says otherwise, though? Some studies give evidence that multitasking damages your productivity, since you never really stay with a task long enough to gain an in-depth understanding. If you value both creativity and productivity, the bottom line may come down to the *kind* of task you're doing. For complex cognitive tasks that require deep understanding and perseverance, it probably pays to hammer away at something, pushing through distractions and encouraging yourself to get in and stay in "the flow." However, if the task you're dealing with is more about creative problem-solving, you may need a different approach.

If you're trying to have a flash of insight, get a clear view of a problem you just can't see, or generate a completely new and unexpected idea, then it may be best to deliberately give yourself a pause in the middle of the process. Turn your brain off by doing something mundane and mentally undemanding, like checking emails or washing the dishes. It only takes a few minutes before you can return to your task with "fresh eyes."

Author Tim Harford has a similar proposition: creative people, he claims, "cross-train" their brains by deliberately doing what he calls "slow-motion multitasking." However, he's careful to make the point that it matters *how* you multitask. It's probably obvious that mindlessly scrolling through social media when you're meant to be working on a project won't benefit you or the project. But by deliberately and consciously switching between many different projects, we may keep our minds fresh and our productivity up. You might have a difficult book you're reading, a work project, a piece of violin music you're tackling or a novel you're working on. You could seamlessly switch between all of these—not out of laziness, avoidance or desperation, but rather governed by our ever-flowing moods with each changing situation.

As we've seen, doing so can give all of these projects a mutual and simultaneous "aha!" moment when you get flashes of insight only after letting something sit and incubate for a while. But you can also derive benefits when you are feeling stuck—sometimes merely contrasting two usually unrelated activities is enough to kick them both into a fresh perspective, jog your creativity or have you looking at the problem in a fresh light. If we define creativity as this ability to apply an idea from one context into another, or the power to mix unexpected ideas together, it's clear why multitasking might facilitate it.

Multitasking strengthens our *fluid intelligence*, which is independent of the content of any task we do. It's about remaining flexible and alert to thinking and creating itself, rather than getting bogged down in any particular details or habits. You "cross-pollinate" your ideas, you expose yourself to multiple sources of potential solutions, and you have more fun, to boot. It turns out that creativity is diametrically opposed to hard work in many ways—it's not about working hard, but working smart. You don't need to slave away with diligence and effort at a task when the right moment of insight is all it takes to elegantly solve the problem.

Make sure that your multitasking is deliberate and conscious, rather than an excuse for procrastination or avoiding challenges. Switch to different tasks to give your brain something fresh and new to work on—and the newness and freshness might very well transfer to other tasks. A writer might find the best way to blast through writer's block is to forget about writing for the afternoon and make soup instead. A manager who's getting nowhere with team negotiations might suddenly get the answer he needs while taking his dog for a walk that afternoon. A sportsman who's "choking" during the game from performance anxiety might find that his game actually improves when he spends less time on the field and more doing his salsa hobby.

Creativity is a dynamic, complex, non-linear thing. It cannot be forced—take a break, get a little messy if need be, take your inspiration where you get it, and don't be afraid to put the task down again to return to later.

Takeaways:

- Rapid idea generation! Welcome to part two with three more techniques for you to plug into your daily life. These techniques are focused more on perspective and process than the prior chapter's.
- First, the six hats method is designed to make you think through six different perspectives. The easiest way to conceptualize these hats is through avatars: Sherlock Holmes (of course!), Sigmund Freud, Eeyore the donkey, a cheerleader, Pablo Picasso, and Henry

Ford. Chances are that's five more perspectives than you would have had otherwise. It's not that each of these hats is creative (they are not), but rather you will find creativity through the combination of these perspectives. All too often we are unable to think outside the box, which is by definition opposing our normal perspectives—this is a framework to do just that.
- Second, creating intentional constraints can force creativity because they require innovation to make something work. It necessitates deviation from the norm, and forces you to rearrange, rethink, repurpose, and reimagine things so basic as definitions and boundaries. There are numerous examples provided, such as dealing with copyright violations, but it can be as simple as asking "What if we had to do things in this certain way?" You'd find a way that is counterintuitive and exploratory by necessity.
- SCAMPER is a tool for creative thinking, as it provides seven distinct ways of approaching a problem or issue: (S) substitute, (C) combine, (A) adapt, (M)

minimize/magnify, (P) put to another use, (E) eliminate, and (R) reverse.
- Finally, what about multitasking? Isn't that something we've always been taught to avoid? Yes, if you're talking about strict productivity, but creativity is a wholly different type of pursuit. When you multitask in a strategic and at least somewhat focused way, you are able to "cross-train" your brain and combine different frameworks, guidelines, mental models, and processes. Creativity can often be stymied when we are stuck in the box, so multitasking takes you outside of the box to view it from another angle.

## Chapter 5: Beyond Convention

It is said that every artist, writer, and innovator has their own creative process. This process constitutes the methods and rituals they use to trigger, maintain, and boost their creative streak so that they produce the most unique and worthwhile outputs by the end of their efforts. For some, the methods are all about consistency, for others it's about sparking a change in perspective, and for others still it's about arousal of the body's adrenaline. It's time that we get innovative about how to reach our own levels of creativity, and you know by this point that there's no easier way to do that than by looking at what others do.

In the earlier parts of this book, we took a peek into the world of Leonardo da Vinci, looking into his habits and ways of thinking that developed his creative mind. There were some very specific patterns of thought that led him to his renown. Now what about other geniuses and masters of their respective crafts? What are the habits and practices that worked to boost their creativity? Can we adopt some of those practices as we try to tackle our own tasks and creative challenges too?

This chapter is all about exploring the creativity methods of famous people from a variety of disciplines—from science and technology to art and literature—so that you can take what you can use and apply it in your own creative endeavors as well. We can learn something from everyone we come across (that's probably a good rule of thumb for life in general), so it behooves us to keep an open mind and explore more unconventional tactics.

## **Einstein and Combinatory Play**

Though Einstein is not traditionally known for his creativity, there can be no doubt that a scientist with outrageous and innovative theories possesses a massive degree of creativity. It's not just following a set of equations that can lead to scientific breakthroughs—a mindset full of openness and finding the unknown is required, and he certainly had those in spades.

You probably know the basics of Einstein's intellectual accomplishments—for instance, the theory of relativity and a newfound understanding of the laws of physics. But you may not know how he was able to come to these discoveries, which were literally unbelievable for the time.

The most notable scientist of the 20th century was known for taking time out of his research to play the violin. Reportedly, he was even very good at it, as he was with the piano. But while sawing away on the violin during his breaks, Einstein actually arrived at some breakthroughs in his research and philosophical questionings. Allegedly one of these musical sessions was the spark for his most famous equation: $E=mc^2$.

Einstein came up with the term "combinatory play" to describe the intangible process in which his favorite pastime led to ideas that revolutionized the whole of scientific thought. He explained his reasoning as best he could in 1945 in a letter to French mathematician Jacques S. Hadamard:

*"My Dear Colleague:*

*In the following, I am trying to answer in brief your questions as well as I am able. I am not satisfied myself with those answers and I am willing to answer more questions if you believe this could be of any advantage for the very interesting and difficult work you have undertaken.*

*(A) The words or the language, as they are written or spoken, do not seem to play any role in my mechanism of thought. The psychical entities which seem to serve as elements in thought are certain signs and more or less clear images which can be 'voluntarily' reproduced and combined.*

*There is, of course, a certain connection between those elements and relevant logical concepts. It is also clear that the desire to arrive finally at logically connected concepts is the emotional basis of this rather vague play with the above-mentioned elements. But taken from a psychological viewpoint, this combinatory play seems to be the essential feature in productive thought—before there is any connection with logical construction in words or other kinds of signs which can be communicated to others.*

*(B) The above-mentioned elements are, in my case, of visual and some of muscular type. Conventional words or other signs have to be sought for laboriously only in a secondary stage, when the mentioned associative play is sufficiently established and can be reproduced at will.*

*(C) According to what has been said, the play with the mentioned elements is aimed to be analogous to certain logical connections one is searching for.*

*(D) Visual and motor. In a stage when words intervene at all, they are, in my case, purely auditive, but they interfere only in a secondary stage, as already mentioned.*

*(E) It seems to me that what you call full consciousness is a limit case which can never be fully accomplished. This seems to be connected with the fact called the*

*narrowness of consciousness (Enge des Bewusstseins)."*

Einstein seemed to believe that indulging in his creative tendencies was helpful for his logical and rational pursuits. That might have been the case, and it also might have been the case that to engage in a distraction was helpful for taking on different perspectives and viewing things from varying angles. Perhaps it's related to the Medici effect from an earlier chapter, in which the melding of different disciplines will inevitably lead to new discoveries.

Indeed, combinatory play is not simply the notion that *play* takes your mind to a different world to regroup. It recognizes, as Einstein did, that taking pieces of knowledge and insight from different disciplines and combining them in new contexts is how most creativity truly happens. So as mentioned, somehow Einstein saw something in playing the violin that helped him think about physics in an entirely new way.

The lesson here is to engage in your own pursuits and not feel constrained by having to stay in similar or adjacent disciplines, thinking that only they will aid you. There are *always* parallels between different disciplines, so find them. More of the same probably will not help; a dash of something different just might.

Einstein became well-known for another thinking technique, and it is one that we use most days in everyday life.

"What if humans were capable of flying?"
"What if the world's landmasses never broke up into separate continents and instead remained as Pangaea to this day?"

These are hypotheticals "what if" questions that tickle your mind into thinking from other perspectives and challenge you to question your premises. Imagining hypotheticals goes beyond simple thinking skills that require only memorization, description of an observable event or situation, or even analysis of facts and concrete events. Because hypotheticals pose questions about what isn't, what hasn't happened, or what isn't likely to ever happen, they challenge the imagination in new ways and sharpen creative thinking and practical intelligence.

For instance, you've never considered the implications of human flight because it's impossible, so there is a world of thoughts that have remained unexplored. How would traffic lights work, what kind of licensing process would be required, would we still have cars and airplanes, and how would safety work? Now, how would those rules and laws apply to normal traffic situations in the present day? Think through the realities of how everything would fit together—it's no small feat!

Hypothetical situations taken to the extreme are thought experiments, and Albert Einstein in particular was known to use these. He called them *Gedankenexperiments*, which is German for "thought experiments."

A thought experiment, in a more general context, is essentially playing out a "what if" scenario to its end. It's acting as if a theory or hypothesis was true, diving deep into the ramifications and seeing what happens to your "what if" scenario under intense scrutiny. A thought experiment allows you to analyze interesting premises you could never achieve in reality and make new leaps of logic and discovery because you can consider possibilities that current knowledge doesn't yet reach.

Suppose the problem situation is needing to exit a room. The conventional ways to do so are to walk out of the door or jump out of the window. But what if the door is blocked by a raging fire and the room is on the tenth floor of the building? These conditions have now rendered your conventional solutions fatal. You can only get out of the room either by finding a way to kill that fire or by having the capacity to survive a fall of several hundred feet. Something in this scenario needs to drastically change its usage or definition, or it will break entirely. This is the essence of the thought experiment. *Suppose this happens. What happens next? And then? And then?*

For example, one of the most famous thought experiments is *Schrödinger's cat*, which was first proposed by physicist Erwin Schrödinger.

In his thought experiment, he sealed a cat inside a box along with two things: a radioactive element and a vial of poison.

There is a 50 percent chance that the radioactive element will decay over the hour, and if it does, then the poison will be released, automatically killing the cat.

But in the 50 percent chance the radioactive element does not decay, the cat will remain alive. Because of the equal probabilities, Schrödinger argued that the cat was simultaneously alive and dead in the box. Without getting into the weeds too much, this is a clear paradox because it is impossible for something to be in two different states simultaneously, being dependent on a random molecular event that wasn't sure to occur.

In other words, the Schrödinger's cat thought experiment proved that there were constraints of current quantum physics theories and certainly gaps in the knowledge of how they were applied. This never could have been something observable or testable, and a simple thought experiment was able to describe it.

Thought experiments were one of Einstein's superpowers. He could imagine a scenario, play it out mentally with shocking accuracy and detail, and then extract the subtle conclusions that lay within.

One of Einstein's most famous *Gedankenexperiments* begins with a simple premise: what would happen if you chased and then eventually caught up with and rode a beam of light through space? In theory, once you caught up to the beam of light, it would appear to be frozen next to you because you are moving at the same speed. Just like if you are walking at the same pace as a car driving next to you, there is no acceleration (the relative velocities are the same), so the car would appear to be stuck to your side.

The only problem was that this was an impossible proposition at the turn of the century. If you catch up to the light and the light appears to be frozen right next to you, then it is inherently impossible for it to be light because of the difference in speeds. It ceases to be light at that moment. This means one of the rules of physics was broken or disproved with this elementary thought.

Therefore, one of the assumptions that underlay physics at the time had to change, and Einstein realized that the assumption of time as a constant needed to shift. This directly laid the path for relativity. The closer you get to the speed the light, the more time becomes different for you—relative to an outside observer.

This thought experiment allowed Einstein to challenge the convention and eventually disprove what were thought to be set-in-stone rules set forth by Isaac Newton's three laws of energy and matter. This thought experiment was instrumental in realizing that people should have questioned old models and fundamental "rules" instead of trying to conform their theories to them.

## **Dali and Chasing Hypnagogic Sleep**

Salvador Dali, best known for his surrealist paintings and perhaps for owning an ocelot as a pet, was one of the first to pursue altered states of consciousness as a means to creativity. He certainly did not know it at the time, but he was capitalizing on a recently discovered function of the brain's different brain waves.

Neuroscientists have recently shined the spotlight on what's known as *theta waves*.

Theta waves are a kind of brain wave present during periods when you're halfway between sleep and wakefulness, or between deep daydreaming and active alertness. During such "theta states," you're not fully awake but not quite asleep either. Such states also include times when you're engaged in such a monotonous or automatic task (e.g., freeway driving, brushing your hair) that you mentally disengage from it and wander into a state that's deeply relaxed but short of sleeping.

According to educator Ned Herrmann, it's during the theta state that people often get good ideas and creative insights, because in such a state, thought censorship is suspended, thoughts move more freely, and creative juices flow more abundantly. It turns out that sleepiness, and in the same vein drunkenness, can actually work wonders for improving your ability to solve problems that require creative insight.

In support of the above notion, author Jonah Lehrer highlights several studies that illustrated how the grogginess of a sleepy or drunk brain can actually improve creative problem-solving ability. In one study, a group of patients with brain injuries resulting in severe attention deficits performed significantly better at solving creatively challenging puzzles compared to normal participants.

Likewise, another study showed that groggy students did better at solving creative problems, and still another study showed similar results after challenging drunk students to tackle such tests. The lack of focus brought on by cognitive deficit, sleepiness, or drunkenness appeared to have allowed the participants a more diffuse way of thinking, such that they were able to consider a wider range of possibilities as their imaginations ran free.

Dali certainly wasn't privy to any of this information, but he espoused a technique he called "slumber with a key" to get himself in such a halfway dream state, also known as *hypnagogic sleep*. In this technique, Dali sits in his chair and holds a key, which is poised just above an upside-down plate. As he dozes off, his hand relaxes and drops the key, which loudly clangs onto the plate and jolts him to wakefulness. Other practitioners of this technique were reportedly Alexander the Great, Thomas Edison, and Albert Einstein as well.

Dali said this practice immersed him to the briefest of naps, not longer than a quarter of a second, and the feeling of having barely lost consciousness for such a fleeting moment revived his physical and psychic being into an immensely creative state. In this way, he kept himself on the edge of consciousness and unconsciousness to effectively reap the rewards of theta waves.

If following Dali's key technique seems a little too dramatic for your taste, there are other methods you can do in daily life to take advantage of that theta or halfway dream state toward improving your flair for problem-solving. Think of the most pressing problem or immediate task you need to accomplish for the day just as you begin to wake in the morning.

Reflect on that concern while your eyes are still closed and your brain still feels a bit dreamy or groggy. During this half-asleep state, let yourself ruminate on a single problem or task without consciously forcing it to take a specific route. Simply allow your mind to sit with that problem. If you happen upon a useful idea or solution in that process, grab a pen and paper or your phone and note down your ideas there so you don't let them slip away into nothingness once you gain full consciousness. Later, revisit these inspired ideas and polish them into a workable solution.

## **Da Vinci and the Habit of Prolific Notes**

Leonardo da Vinci, an epitome of the prolific creative, had this simple but effective creativity method: prolific notetaking. Over his lifetime, he accumulated about 13,000 pages of notes and sketches—that's 13,000 pages each written out by hand. Of those, an estimated 7,000 pages are preserved, like surviving snapshots of the inner workings of a creative genius's mind. They were filled with drawings of imagined inventions, diagrams of human and animal anatomy, and personal notes and observations that were often written backward—so da Vinci could add a small layer of secrecy to his inner thoughts.

Wherever he went, da Vinci always carried paper on which he could immediately jot down his passing thoughts, sights he noticed all around him, impressions and observations, information from people he admired, jokes that amused him, and drawings of his visions and imaginings. Many of the pages he filled had a simple sketch at the center, a label on top, arrows signifying major content, annotations along the margins, and sometimes a summary at the bottom.

Da Vinci also did most of his sketches on individual sheets of paper, which allowed him greater freedom to experiment with mixing and matching different pages together. In the process, he got to connect, reconnect, and group together ideas, facts, and observations in both familiar and unusual ways, helping enhance his creative eye even more.

Notetaking significantly aided da Vinci's creativity because by writing things down, he kept his observations, ideas, insights, and even passing thoughts always present and available for his perusal. He could take an observation from a previous year and pair it with something from his morning, and it would clarify his thoughts. Even though those observations or thoughts might not have seemed that significant when he wrote them, it mattered a lot that he noted them down and preserved them in those pages.

Some of them were certainly trivial and unimportant but were recorded anyway—this is an important point, for we only know what is trivial in hindsight, so we *should* be writing everything .

Sometimes ideas just need to be preserved and kept on hold for a time, until you encounter a situation later on that would be the perfect opportunity for that idea to be applied. Da Vinci made sure he didn't let an observation or idea go to waste, and such a habit made all the difference. So if you want to boost your creativity, take a leaf out of da Vinci's book—and write notes on it. It may feel like you're not accomplishing anything at first, but the key is to wait until you have a certain number of notes to draw back on. That's when this effect gets amplified, much like compound interest on a bank savings account.

A library with two books is not such a great resource, but a library with two hundred books can start to become a formidable repository of information.

## **Murakami and King and Living Through Routines**

Another creativity-boosting method many artists swear by is having a daily routine and sticking with it. As we've seen in the previous chapters, great ideas often come while you're hard at work, not while you're sitting around and waiting for inspiration to strike you before you get moving. You provide the best chance for creativity to flourish when you stick to a routine that preps and stimulates your mind to get creative, as attested to by renowned authors Haruki Murakami and Stephen King.

Haruki Murakami is a Japanese author who typically writes short stories that are both poignant and offer insight into the human condition. Many of his books have been adapted into plays and movies. Stephen King, on the other hand, is an American author best known for his imaginative horror novels—whether you know it or not, you have probably watched one of his books that has been adapted into a movie screenplay. By the way, together, they have sold close to one billion books, so there must be something that they are doing correctly.

The degree to which they abide by their daily writing routines is almost coordinated, but it just so happens to be what works for these two prolific writers.

Murakami and King both follow an ironclad daily routine to get them in the best condition for writing. Every day, Murakami consistently gets up at 4:00 a.m., works for five to six hours, and then goes for either a ten-kilometer run, a 1500-meter swim, or both in the afternoon. He then does some reading and listens to music and goes to bed at 9:00 p.m. every night. Murakami says the repetition of this daily routine, without variation, is central to his creative process. He considers this routine a way to mesmerize himself to get into a deeper state of mind, unlocking his creative potentials and awakening his artistic sensitivity as a writer.

Though Murakami never says as much, from a bystander perspective, it seems as if he is saving all his mental juice for his work at the expense of the variety in his life. This has some scientific support in the concept of *decision fatigue*—the continued weakening of our ability to ponder decisions as the day goes on.

King has a similar method for tapping his creativity in writing. He believes that if you stick to a schedule, then you habituate yourself to certain ways of being and thinking. For example, going to bed at the same hour and sleeping the same amount each night trains your body to expect sleep at that hour and for that duration. In the same way, King says, you can train your waking mind to work creatively by establishing a routine around it, such as by going in your writing room at around the same time each day and leaving your writing desk once you're done putting out a thousand words for the day.

King himself has a routine when it comes to writing: he sits down in the same seat, at about the same time each morning (8:00–8:30), with a glass of water or a cup of tea, his vitamin pill, his music, and his papers all arranged in the same places. He says that consistently doing this same routine every day is a way of prepping his mind to have the waking dreams that lead to successful fiction stories—a way of telling his mind, "You're going to be dreaming soon."

In addition to Murakami and King, many other prominent writers have each developed their own unique customs and habits to get their creative juices flowing. Virginia Woolf spent her twenties writing two and a half hours each morning on a 3.5-foot-tall standing desk with an angled top, enabling her to view her writings both up-close and from afar. John Steinbeck always had exactly twelve perfectly sharpened pencils on his desk to ensure he never had to disrupt his creative flow just to replenish his writing materials. Agatha Christie had the habit of mulling over murder plots while crunching on apples in the bathtub. Anthony Trollope started his day at 5:30 a.m. sharp and strictly stuck to the routine of writing 250 words every fifteen minutes.

Some of these routines begin to sound more like superstitions, but perhaps that is part of their effectiveness. If you engage in a certain set of actions and behaviors, you believe that a certain outcome is likely to happen. And so you cause it to happen.

Whatever the case, creativity doesn't just come out of nowhere. It is routines that stimulate and set the stage for its arrival. Having a routine of your own is like dusting off the sofa, plumping up its cushions, putting out snacks on the coffee table, and inviting creativity over like a friend you want to spend hours and hours with, just bonding and enjoying good conversation together. In other words, routines make it easier for creativity to come sit with you and stay with you when you need it to. When you build a habit around working on that creative task every day, regardless of how motivated or inspired you feel, creativity becomes more of a natural outcome to an honest day's work instead of some elusive ideal you have to keep chasing after.

## Dr. NakaMats, the Most Unconventional of All

The connection between the mind and the body is another important factor to consider when trying to get more creative. Creativity can be sparked by methods that stimulate the physical body, and while this is unconventional, it has one powerful proponent. One of the best proofs of the mind-body connection is exemplified by the creative process of inventor Dr. Yoshiro Nakamatsu, better known as Dr. NakaMats. Dr. NakaMats is the inventor of the floppy disk—and several thousand other gadgets and gizmos, including the CD, the DVD, the karaoke machine, the fax machine, fuel-cell-powered boots, the world's tiniest air conditioner, and a self-defense wig, among others. With 3,300 patents to his name, Dr. NakaMats is an embodiment of the prolific creative. His creativity method? Oxygen deprivation.

To spark his creative thoughts, Dr. NakaMats goes on long underwater swims, diving deep and holding his breath for as long as he can in order to starve his brain of oxygen. He warns that too much oxygen in the brain inhibits inspiration from striking, so the key to boosting inventiveness is to limit the oxygen available to the brain. He reports that by forcing himself to stop his breathing underwater, he gets to visualize an invention half a second before death. At that point, he notes the idea down on a proprietary waterproof notepad, then comes up to the surface with an all-new project in mind.

It was by depriving his body of oxygen that Dr. NakaMats was able to jolt an idea from his brain. You may raise your eyebrow at this, but it's undeniable that some aspect of this process assisted Dr. NakaMats in some way. In instances where someone is as much of an outlier as Dr. NakaMats is, and he also uses an outlier of a technique, they may very well be connected.

But while Dr. NakaMats uses oxygen deprivation to stimulate his inventiveness, on the other end of the spectrum are creatives who try to boost their creativity via methods that improve oxygen circulation throughout their body. One such tactic is exercise, which fosters healthy blood flow and better oxygen delivery to different parts of the body, including the brain. With increased oxygen supply, the brain has an improved capacity to carry out its activities, including the cognitive efforts required in the process of creativity.

For instance, a 2014 Stanford University study found that walking significantly improved convergent thinking and divergent thinking, which are cognitive processes essential to creativity. Other studies have shown that in those who exercise at least three times a week, convergent thinking is significantly improved.

Thus, thinkers and artists who use exercise as a creativity method are obviously on to something. History's notable thinkers Henry David Thoreau, Jean-Jacques Rousseau, Immanuel Kant, and Friedrich Nietzsche all had a habit of theorizing while walking. Celebrated author Ernest Hemingway boxed, novelist Haruki

Murakami loves running, and writer Kathy Acker engaged in bodybuilding. Guido van der Werve, a Dutch artist and composer, competes in triathlons and attests that going for a run makes him sharper and improves his focus and concentration.

So evidently, oxygen has some effect on creativity. But how could two seemingly opposite methods—depriving your brain of oxygen and improving oxygen supply to your brain via exercise—both improve your creativity? The answer may have something to do with adrenaline. Adrenaline is a hormone produced by your body when you are in a state of stress, whether physical, mental, or even imagined. Increased demands on the body, such as an emergency situation, trigger an adrenaline boost, which helps you cope with the stress by making you quicker, stronger, and sharper. Forcing an oxygen shortage in your system (as Dr. NakaMats does) and increasing oxygen supply by physical exertion both put your body in a stressed state. This, in turn, elicits an adrenaline rush.

With more adrenaline in your system, you get to enjoy enhanced perceptiveness, a better ability to think of new ways you can use existing resources, and a sharpened capacity to make new connections—all of which produce a boost in your creativity.

## **Edison and Why Nothing is Sacred**

Thomas Edison is a household name to most of us, but in the world of innovation and invention, he is the paragon to which people aspire. He had 1,093 patents to his name for products that included the phonograph, alkaline storage battery, typewriter, and motion picture camera, among others. Of course, he is best known for the lightbulb. The 3,500 notebooks he left when he passed away tell the story of how an early conception evolves into a full-fledged invention in the mind of a legendary innovator. What follows are two of the strategies Edison used to facilitate such creative process in his brain and become one of the most famous inventors in history.

First, Edison set idea quotas for himself and the rest of his workers. He believed in first going for quantity of ideas in order to create the best chance for a high-quality concept to come through in the midst of all those others. Edison himself aimed to come up with one major invention every six months and one minor invention every ten days. If you imagine that an idea has a 1 percent chance of becoming a successful invention, then imagine how many ideas must be generated every ten days! This mindset is no surprise, coming from the person who brought us the famous quote about genius being 1 percent inspiration and 99 percent perspiration. He also brought us a quote about discovering 10,000 incorrect ways to invent the light bulb. Edison believed in prolific, hard work, and creativity as a secondary thought.

He was not fazed, no matter how many of his ideas turned out to be flops; all that mattered to him was that he kept on generating as many ideas as he could until he produced a good one that actually worked. This method was highly effective in improving his creativity, as it made sure that all surface-level ideas—which are often safe, familiar, and common ones—got purged out first, clearing the way for fresher perspectives and more imaginative innovations to come through.

This is quite similar to what we discussed earlier with rapid idea generation and the section about generating a hundred ideas. Once you are past the low-hanging fruit and everything that appears relevant and related, that's when the actual creative work begins.

Secondly, Edison had the habit of challenging assumptions. He questioned common beliefs and was not afraid to try anything out of the ordinary. He believed that his lack of formal education was a blessing, as it allowed him more freedom to innovate without being constrained by suppositions, traditional views, and dogma taught in schools.

Edison approached every project with fewer assumptions and fewer preconceived notions about what's possible, and this mindset enabled him to better expand his thinking and connect elements people originally thought were incompatible. It was his habit of being open to a variety of perspectives and seeing nature in all its great possibilities that helped Edison become the prolific inventor that he was.

As you can see, there is a wide variety of methods that creatives employ to tap their creative juices. Some induce certain physical states such as hypnagogic sleep or an adrenaline rush from either oxygen deprivation or an oxygen boost from physical exercise. Others practice habits such as notetaking or sticking with a daily routine.

Still others challenge their minds to combine things, come up with as many ideas as possible, and challenge assumptions. These are all techniques tested and proven by the masters themselves. Take your pick, then practice it yourself—and discover how much more creative you can be.

Takeaways:

- Of course, we've stated that nothing is original and all creativity is derivative in some way, so why can't the creativity techniques we use also be so? This chapter is dedicated to examining the techniques and routines of some of history's most prolific creatives so you can steal what works for you. You already know the conventional ways to generate creativity, so how about thinking outside the box to think outside the box?

- We would be remiss if we didn't discuss Albert Einstein. Though he's known for his achievements in science, a certain degree of creativity is certainly needed for scientific breakthroughs. He used two tactics to great success: combinatory play (intersperse creative and logical pursuits to try to subconsciously draw parallels) and thought experiments (playing out hypotheticals to their logical end). The former mixes different types of thinking to become greater than the sum of two parts, and the latter helps you imagine that which literally does not or cannot exist in reality.
- Salvador Dali was known for his mustache, his art, and his ocelot Babou. He also became known for chasing hypnagogic sleep, which is that fine line between sleep and consciousness. It's in this elusive zone that he claimed to find

his most creative thoughts. He got there by using his key-in-the-hand technique, which is done by falling asleep while holding a key in his hand, upon which point he would drop the key, which would cause a noise that would wake him, thus keeping him in the hypnagogic zone.

- Da Vinci has more up his sleeve for us! In addition to everything we have covered about his proclivities and mindsets, he was one of the most prolific notetakers in history. This allowed him to cross-reference his own thoughts and observations and build upon them without losing a beat. He eventually created his own mental library in his notebooks. Not every thought we have is brilliant, but when you are able to combine and reflect, you can often use yourself as a resource.
- Haruki Murakami and Stephen King are bestselling authors—quite an understatement. They both use routines to an exacting degree. Murakami seems to want to preserve his mental powers for his creativity, while King theorized that you could condition the brain to exist in a mode of creativity with enough

repetition. For both, it is clear that they've developed specific work modes that help them focus and concentrate on the task at hand.

- Dr. NakaMats is a Japanese inventor who you might call insane. His method of reaching creativity is oxygen deprivation through swimming. It's possible that this is similar to Dali's method of chasing hypnagogic sleep and being in a state of semi-consciousness, wherein the brain generates different brain waves. Other creatives have espoused exercise—which also adds an element of oxygen deprivation (if sufficiently strenuous). The common thread of elevated adrenaline might be what's at work here.
- Finally, Thomas Edison, inventor of the lightbulb, ran a workshop of invention. He truly approached creativity like a business—he believed in quantity over quality, and that's why he ended up with so many patents. However, he also tended to challenge assumptions and conventional knowledge, seeing them as arbitrary and limiting to the purpose of creativity and freer thought.

**Summary Guide**

## Chapter 1. Introduction

- Creativity is something we all want, but how can we even define it? Perhaps we can describe it best by looking at someone who appeared to embody creativity—Leonardo da Vinci. He possessed a few traits in spades that may have been the keys to his success: curiosity, experimentation, mindfulness, embracing the unknown, and balancing multiple disciplines in both artistic and scientific endeavors alike. We can emulate these traits, which means creativity is a learnable quality. The spark of insight that James Dyson used to create his revolutionary vacuum cleaner was a distillation of some of those traits.

- Some of us, however, are constrained by one of the most longstanding myths in psychology—the myth of hemisphere-specific functionality. In other words, people believe that they have talent in only the left hemisphere (logic, rationality) or the right hemisphere (creativity, art). This leads us to believe that we are inherently destined for a lack of creativity. Basic neurobiology proves this to be untrue. Moreover, three specific modes of thought all span both hemispheres. We're all two-hemisphere thinkers!

- There have often been associations between creativity and mental illness. Do these claims hold any water? Yes and no. There is certainly a correlation between the two groups, but there is nothing to suggest that one causes the other. A major factor may be the functioning of the precuneus, a brain structure that filters out mental chatter from your consciousness. Thus, if it filters poorly, your head will be filled with endless chatter that you can't turn off. This can be fertile ground for creative ideas just as easily as "insanity" from not being able to experience silence.

- We already know we want creativity, but it also has health benefits. Creativity has been shown to reduce stress, improve brain functioning, and create similar soothing effects to meditation. This is achieved through keeping an active brain.

- Last and certainly not least, creativity gives you the tools and keys to solve problems. This might seem self-evident, but it's not always that we need creative *solutions*; sometimes we need to creatively define the *problem* as well. We frequently will need to look at matters from a completely different perspective to get where we want.

## Chapter 2. Creativity Building Blocks

- We learned that Leonardo da Vinci abided by some strict mindsets in his quest to be creatively prolific. This chapter contains some building blocks and builds upon those mindsets, while seeking to dispel some myths surrounding creativity that might be holding you back.
- It's helpful to first explore what keeps us from being creative, what keeps us

inside the box, and what keeps us from tapping into our inner well of ideas and zaniness. Roger Von Oech calls these barriers mental locks, and they are all internal dialogues that are at odds with creative thinking and rapid idea generation. In essence, they make us think too safely and conventionally, while controlled by a healthy amount of self-doubt and self-consciousness.

- First, nothing is new. Everything is derivative. Most things are merely a result of being adjacent possible. And this is a good thing! Take the pressure off yourself to completely reinvent and revolutionize, and then redirect your attention to what already exists and how you can use it for yourself. Simply look around first before sequestering yourself in a quest to be 100 percent innovative.
- Second, inspiration is a myth. There is no muse. There is no flash of insight or epiphany. These things do not exist. Well, at least plan for life without these things because you cannot control them. Thus, approach creativity as a skill you must cultivate, and practice it like any

other skill. Key to this is gaining confusion endurance.
- Third, creativity comes from combinations of element. This is called the Medici effect. What is commonplace in one field might just be revolutionary in another, so again, redirect your attention to what is plainly visible already instead of seeking a moonshot.
- Fourth, psychological distance is necessary for creativity because when we leave too much of ourselves in a thought process, we become constrained by arbitrary and unnecessary limitations. We are also unable to break out of certain perspectives, whether through habit, emotional investment, or reinforcement.

## Chapter 3. Rapid Idea Generation

- Ideas are a valuable resource that can determine your fate, whether it's your career or how comfortable you are on your couch. While we can utilize some of the creativity building blocks, there are specific techniques to generate more ideas in less time. Generating ideas out of thin air is difficult, so it always helps to have methods to organize the fog that is your brain.

- First, shoot for a hundred ideas. This sounds like madness, but there is a method to the madness. Often, ideas are difficult because we are stuck along one line of thought. You're in your box. Trying for one hundred forces you to think differently and abandon lines of thought. It pushes you into a zone of absurdity and "why not?" and that's more or less where thinking outside the box begins.
- Second, make friends with randomization. This can take the form of playing *shiritori*, using the alphabet, forcing relationships between random objects, random input, creating and using Harvey cards, and giving clustering (similar to mind maps) a shot.
- Third, try to let go of the emotions and attachments you place on things and think more plainly. Consider problems more generally as opposed to specifically, and try to get away from the negative effects of functional fixedness.
- Finally, systematically create combinations with an idea box.

## Chapter 4. Rapid Idea Generation Part 2

- Rapid idea generation! Welcome to part two with three more techniques for you to plug into your daily life. These techniques are focused more on perspective and process than the prior chapter's.
- First, the six hats method is designed to make you think through six different perspectives. The easiest way to conceptualize these hats is through avatars: Sherlock Holmes (of course!), Sigmund Freud, Eeyore the donkey, a cheerleader, Pablo Picasso, and Henry Ford. Chances are that's five more perspectives than you would have had otherwise. It's not that each of these hats is creative (they are not), but rather you will find creativity through the combination of these perspectives. All too often we are unable to think outside the box, which is by definition opposing our normal perspectives—this is a framework to do just that.
- Second, creating intentional constraints can force creativity because they require innovation to make something work. It necessitates deviation from the norm,

and forces you to rearrange, rethink, repurpose, and reimagine things so basic as definitions and boundaries. There are numerous examples provided, such as dealing with copyright violations, but it can be as simple as asking "What if we had to do things in this certain way?" You'd find a way that is counterintuitive and exploratory by necessity.

- SCAMPER is a tool for creative thinking, as it provides seven distinct ways of approaching a problem or issue: (S) substitute, (C) combine, (A) adapt, (M) minimize/magnify, (P) put to another use, (E) eliminate, and (R) reverse.
- Finally, what about multitasking? Isn't that something we've always been taught to avoid? Yes, if you're talking about strict productivity, but creativity is a wholly different type of pursuit. When you multitask in a strategic and at least somewhat focused way, you are able to "cross-train" your brain and combine different frameworks, guidelines, mental models, and processes. Creativity can often be stymied when we are stuck in the box, so

multitasking takes you outside of the box to view it from another angle.

## Chapter 5: Beyond Convention

- Of course, we've stated that nothing is original and all creativity is derivative in some way, so why can't the creativity techniques we use also be so? This chapter is dedicated to examining the techniques and routines of some of history's most prolific creatives so you can steal what works for you. You already know the conventional ways to generate creativity, so how about thinking outside the box to think outside the box?
- We would be remiss if we didn't discuss Albert Einstein. Though he's known for his achievements in science, a certain degree of creativity is certainly needed for scientific breakthroughs. He used two tactics to great success: combinatory play (intersperse creative and logical pursuits to try to subconsciously draw parallels) and thought experiments (playing out hypotheticals to their logical end). The former mixes different types of thinking

to become greater than the sum of two parts, and the latter helps you imagine that which literally does not or cannot exist in reality.

- Salvador Dali was known for his mustache, his art, and his ocelot Babou. He also became known for chasing hypnagogic sleep, which is that fine line between sleep and consciousness. It's in this elusive zone that he claimed to find his most creative thoughts. He got there by using his key-in-the-hand technique, which is done by falling asleep while holding a key in his hand, upon which point he would drop the key, which would cause a noise that would wake him, thus keeping him in the hypnagogic zone.
- Da Vinci has more up his sleeve for us! In addition to everything we have covered about his proclivities and mindsets, he was one of the most prolific notetakers in history. This allowed him to cross-reference his own thoughts and observations and build upon them without losing a beat. He eventually created his own mental library in his notebooks. Not every thought we have is brilliant, but when you are able to

combine and reflect, you can often use yourself as a resource.
- Haruki Murakami and Stephen King are bestselling authors—quite an understatement. They both use routines to an exacting degree. Murakami seems to want to preserve his mental powers for his creativity, while King theorized that you could condition the brain to exist in a mode of creativity with enough repetition. For both, it is clear that they've developed specific work modes that help them focus and concentrate on the task at hand.
- Dr. NakaMats is a Japanese inventor who you might call insane. His method of reaching creativity is oxygen deprivation through swimming. It's possible that this is similar to Dali's method of chasing hypnagogic sleep and being in a state of semi-consciousness, wherein the brain generates different brain waves. Other creatives have espoused exercise—which also adds an element of oxygen deprivation (if sufficiently strenuous). The common thread of elevated adrenaline might be what's at work here.

- Finally, Thomas Edison, inventor of the lightbulb, ran a workshop of invention. He truly approached creativity like a business—he believed in quantity over quality, and that's why he ended up with so many patents. However, he also tended to challenge assumptions and conventional knowledge, seeing them as arbitrary and limiting to the purpose of creativity and freer thought.

www.ingramcontent.com/pod-product-compliance
Lightning Source LLC
Chambersburg PA
CBHW071344080526
44587CB00017B/2953